THAT DAY

A Memoir of Eight Siblings
Separated by a Broken Family

THAT DAY

A Memoir of Eight Siblings
Separated by a Broken Family

Richard C. Burt

HenschelHAUS Publishing, Inc.
Milwaukee, Wisconsin

Published by
HenschelHAUS Publishing, Inc.
www.henschelHAUSbooks.com
Milwaukee, Wisconsin

ISBN: 978159598-945-1
LCCN: 2022952105

Printed in the United States of America

I dedicate this book to all of my siblings:

- *Jackie*
- *Marlene*
- *Judy*
- *Ron*
- *Kathy*
- *Allen (Tom)*
- *Janet*
- *Joy*

TABLE OF CONTENTS

Chapter 1

ROB'S VISIT

LIKE MOST PEOPLE, MY LIFE HAS had ups and downs. I was born into a large family, but raised as an only child. I was three years old when I experienced THAT DAY. However, now looking back on my life, I actually had five THAT DAYs that significantly changed my life. I feel very lucky to be where I am today considering the possibilities for my life had THAT DAY not happened.

At the age of 71, I am enjoying my comfortable, retired life in Hendersonville surrounded by the beautiful Blue Ridge Mountains of western North Carolina in the eastern part of the United States. It is a small city—population about 15,000. The weather fluctuates through four distinct seasons; however, the climate is moderate—does not change drastically as in other parts of our country.

Before European settlers arrived here, the Cherokee were the native Americans. However, in 1830, the federal government forced MOST of them (some hid out in the mountains) to walk a "Trail of Tears" west across the Mississippi River to establish a reservation, now in Oklahoma. They now call themselves the "Western Band." That was a dark day in our nation's history. The natives who remained in NC call themselves the "Eastern Band."

In the past few years, "craft beer" brewing has become a significant industry in the surrounding areas. Traditionally, Henderson County has been known for three things: tourism, apple orchards, and kudzu. In September, Hendersonville celebrates a four-day Apple Festival that occupies over six blocks up and down Main Street. Kudzu is a ubiquitous, wild-growing, invasive vine that crawls up telephone poles and covers trees in the summer.

I am still single—never married—and have no children. A few years ago, arthritis in both hips and lower back convinced me to stop bicycling and running—no fun anymore. I still try to walk and stretch every day, and still desire to play recreational competitive tennis, but arthritis stiffness limits my court time to mostly coaching junior kids. Coaching is my effort to "give back" for all the help that I got as a kid. I try to make tennis FUN for the kids— great fun for me to see the smiles on their fresh faces. I am not a licensed professional instructor—volunteer coach. I try to emphasize good footwork on the court. I want to see "Happy Feet." I consider myself a "student of the game."

I frequently view YouTube videos on tennis instruction. I have read several books on tennis history, and I subscribe to *TENNIS* magazine. I am a life member of the United States Tennis Association. I am also an active member of the local Community Tennis Association to promote youth tennis. When I am not on the courts with kids, I enjoy volunteering for several local non-profit activities, and I read often now (not much when I was younger), and frequently visit the public library.

Henderson County has an excellent system of library branches. In the winter, I often visit the Etowah branch to enjoy the sunlight exposure through the large south-facing windows of the modern building design. However, I mostly visit the Hendersonville, main branch—besides a wide variety of books, magazines and newspapers, it offers 20-some up-to-date computers for public use. (I have no computer at my apartment—I enjoy going to my "office" at the library).

In my youth, I never visited a public library until I was in high school. My parents never encouraged me to read. However, now in retirement, reading helps to pass the time.

At the library one day, I sat down to a computer. I logged into my Google account to check my emails. Most of them were solicitations for political or non-profit donations. Some were ads from nutritional supplement companies. One email was from ROB. Who is Rob I thought—tennis friend, tennis parent, non-profit staffer? I am careful these days to open strange emails because of phishing, etc. Then it hit me—my nephew in Racine, Wisconsin!

Rob is my oldest brother's son. Rob married in the summer of the year that I moved from Racine to Hendersonville—15 years ago. I was introduced to his bride, Sarah, at their wedding reception held at the Kenosha Country Club. I had mostly lost touch with family and friends in Wisconsin, except for occasional greeting cards and emails. Rob and Sarah now had a 13-year-old son who would like to meet their Uncle Rick. They are planning a summer trip to Charleston, SC to visit friends and would like to stop through Hendersonville to visit me.

"Will you be available for our visit?"

"Absolutely," I replied. "Nice to hear from you. I will be available for your visit. Please bring swimsuits if you want to visit some waterfalls, which are plentiful in the area. I look forward to seeing you."

They arrived in Hendersonville late one afternoon and called me. I drove to their motel, near the interstate highway, about five miles from downtown. I live near, but on the opposite side of town. I was thinking, *where should I take them for dinner?* Near their motel is a Zaxby's restaurant.

When Rob opened the room door, a very warm, exhilarating feeling overcame me. He is taller than me. We hugged. Sarah was still drying her hair from a shower, but nevertheless gave me a hug. Their son, Ronnie, shook my hand—our first meeting. We sat down and reminisced about family history. Sarah noticed the time and suggested that we get to a restaurant. I suggested the Zaxby's restaurant nearby. They said that they had picked up the Hendersonville tourist magazine in the motel lobby. They had noticed a restaurant called "Postero" located on Main Street in downtown, and made a reservation. Ok with me.

The restaurant is located in an old bank building with two floors. It was crowded—good thing we had reservations. We enjoyed a nice meal and shared more family memories. We were ones of the last patrons to leave. Before leaving, Rob and Sarah visited the restrooms. On their way, they passed the manager's office—the original bank vault. Rob thought that was neat. Back at the motel, we sat in the lobby for a while and discussed plans for the next day. I suggested that we visit DuPont State Recreational Forest—about a 10-mile drive.

The next morning, I met them again at their motel. I brought four bath towels, bottled water, and snacks. We piled into their rented SUV — Rob drove and I navigated. However, Rob accessed the car's GPS system to check on my directions. From the forest parking lot, we hiked to the first view called "Hooker Falls." I suggested that we must enjoy the water. I jumped into the cool water. Sarah waded in. Rob got his feet wet. Ronnie got his toes wet. We returned to the car for drinks.

Then we headed out on the longer trail hike to "Triple Falls." I mentioned that I was not sure if the arthritis in my hips and back would allow me to keep up with them, but I would try. However, I think that adrenaline from their presence helped me to walk okay and enjoy the outing. They took lots of photos. The falls are really stunning. I again jumped in the cool water. Sarah waded in, Rob dipped his feet, while Ronnie sat on the large rocks and watched.

Back at their motel, we said goodbye. I sent them on their way to visit Asheville (about 20 miles away) before catching a flight back to Wisconsin.

The next day, I emailed my older sister Marlene in Racine about Rob's visit:

"Rob, Sarah, and Ronnie visited me. I do not get many visitors—I thoroughly enjoyed seeing them. We reminisced about our family history. Great to see Rob. Sarah is a real sweet lady. Rob is so lucky. I am very jealous! It was my first time with Ronnie. We took a hike to see nearby waterfalls. They took lots of photos—hopefully, they will visit you and share them. After they left for Asheville, I thought about OUR life. Marlene, You have sent me lots of family history information. Have YOU ever considered writing about OUR life history?"

Over the years, I have mentioned bits and pieces of my life story to several people. The typical response has been, "Wow, you have an interesting story. You should write a book!" Me, write a book? Sure! Reading and writing were never my strengths in school. I consider myself sufficiently literate. However, as I have gotten older, I am much better at both. My adopted parents often told me how much they enjoyed my letter stories to them. Of course, parents are biased. However, now I am thinking about a book. So, at age 71, with the help of family members, I decided to take on the challenge—perhaps mostly for self-therapy and healing.

This book is a story of a large poor family, a broken home, divorce, separated siblings, foster families, adoption, re-connection and changes to my hometown—Racine, Wisconsin, in the midwestern part of the United States. This has been an emotional journey for me. You may find some parts of the story difficult to believe. I hope that you find it interesting and entertaining.

Chapter 2
RACINE ON THE LAKE

I LIVED ON AND OFF FOR 31 YEARS IN RACINE. It is a moderately sized, Midwestern city in southeastern Wisconsin on the shore of Lake Michigan, and divided by the Root River. Racine is located about 20 miles south of Milwaukee. About 10 miles further south is Kenosha. Then, another 60 miles south is Chicago. With the help of the Internet and Wikipedia, I will present my thoughts of Wisconsin and my hometown.

Wisconsin is known by two nicknames: "America's Dairyland," and the "Badger State." The word "Wisconsin" is derived from a combination of Native and French meanings for "Gathering of the Waters"—over 15,000 inland lakes, and over 12,000 rivers and streams. It is a beautiful state. However, the weather is challenging: Winter days can be very cold (I experienced 25 degrees below zero Fahrenheit), windy with lots of snow and ice; summer days can be hot, humid, and windy with lots of flying insects. The state bird is the robin, but I think it should be the mosquito!

Did I mention wind? Along the lakeshore, it is always windy. Many places in the state experience average wind speeds exceeding 20 miles per hour! That is great for sailboating. However, in summer, wind is real challenging if one wishes to enjoy tennis or bicycling. In winter, wind with cold temperatures is not fun for trying to enjoy a walk. I often observed the condensing white plume of the stack gases, usually traveling horizontally with the wind rather than vertically, from the nearby coal-fired power plant.

The worst consequence of high wind that I ever observed was in 1999 when the "Big Blue" crane collapsed during construction of the new stadium (initially called Miller Park, but now American Family Field) to replace the original County Stadium for the Milwaukee Brewers baseball team. The disaster resulted in the death of three ironworkers and delayed construction about a year.

Early Wisconsin was occupied by many Native American tribes, including the Ho-chunk, Ojibway, Menominee, Winnebago, Fox, Sauk, and Potawatomi. In the 1600s, several French explorers crossed Lake Michigan and landed in what is now known as Green Bay. Among these explorers were Nicolet, Joliet and Marquette—names that are prevalent around the state. Famous naturalists were Aldo Leopold, John Muir, and Governor / US Senator Gaylord Nelson, who organized the first Earth Day celebration in 1970. The most prominent architect was Frank Lloyd Wright.

In the early 1800s, native Fox and Sauk men in the Southwest part of the State, under contract with the

Federal Government, began to supplement hunting with mining, and shipped lead ore to the East Coast. Later, European lead miners moved in. Because of the lack of trees, they dug their homes into the sides of the hills, like "badgers." This fact always seemed bizarre to me, because most of the rest of Wisconsin is flat and covered with trees. Badgers are short-legged animals with flat, wide (squat) bodies and heavy claws for digging. They shelter underground, living in burrows.

As settlement grew, agriculture became a major business. The soil is mostly black—rich in organic matter, with a mixture of sand, clay, and carbonates. The official state soil is called "Antigo Silt Loam."

Today, Wisconsin has over 60,000 farms; about 40,000 are dairy farms, with over one million cows. In the summer, you can see thousands of acres of field corn that is grown as "silage" to feed the cows. All dairy farms have at least one tall, cylindrical silo next to the typical red barn for silage storage. In addition, field corn is now a major raw material for ethanol fuel production. Many farms grow a variety of vegetables, mostly cabbage, cranberries, ginseng, peas, potatoes, snap beans, soybeans and sweet corn. Maple syrup is also a valuable natural commodity—tapped from sugar maple trees.

Wild rice is another of Wisconsin's natural resources. For thousands of years, it has been a prized food source and important cultural and spiritual component of native tribal ceremonies. Today, harvesting of both wild rice and ginseng are strictly regulated by the Wisconsin Department of Natural Resources (DNR).

Wisconsin is particularly famous for its cheese and beer. I grew up eating lots of bratwurst, coleslaw, sauerkraut, German potato salad, sweet corn on the cob, and of course, many cheeses. I prefer Muenster; string cheese is handy for bicycling and hiking. My adopted dad preferred limburger—aged, stinky cheese, along with a few beers. Sunday breakfast was always pancakes with maple syrup. On Fridays, fried yellow perch from Lake Michigan was popular for lunch and/or dinner.

The Wisconsin populations of two large bird species have recovered nicely with supportive efforts from the Wisconsin Department of Natural Resources (DNR) in last few years: sandhill cranes and bald eagles. The cranes are migratory birds, flying south in the winter.

Recreational fishing has always been popular in Lake Michigan, especially for yellow perch and smelt. In 1829, the Welland Canal opened as a bypass around Niagara Falls, allowing direct access for ocean ships from the St. Lawrence River to the Great Lakes. The result was a great expansion in commercial fishing on the Great Lakes, including herring, lake trout, yellow perch, and whitefish.

RACINE

In 1834, a Lake Michigan seaman, Captain Gilbert Knapp, founded a settlement called "Port Gilbert" in Southeast Wisconsin, where the Potawatomi natives lived. The settlement name was later changed to "Racine," the French word for "root." Racine has been known by several nicknames: Belle City of the Lakes, Kringle Capital of America, Kringleville, and Invention City.

I have never read any reference as to why has Racine been referred to as "Belle City," just that the label is prominent around the area—apartment names, business names, community names, etc. Even the Racine Heritage Museum has no clear reference, except that writers in the 1840s frequently spoke of the beauty of Racine and its surroundings. *Belle* is the French word for beautiful. One high school history teacher told me that he heard a rumor that Lake Michigan sailors and commercial fishermen who visited Racine thought that the Main Street buildings had attractive designs, and that the girls of Racine were cute.

Racine was settled by waves of immigrants from many European countries: Germany, Denmark, Norway, Bohemia, England, Czechoslovakia, Poland, Ireland, Italy, and Lithuania. Large numbers of African Americans, and people from Mexico and Latin America also migrated to Racine. Racine has a large statue in a prominent location of one of its early community leaders and statesmen, Karel Jonas. He came to Racine from Bohemia (now part of the Czech Republic in central Europe) in1863. He established and edited the first known Czech newspaper in the U.S. He later served on the Racine Common Council, was elected to the State Assembly, then to the State Senate, and finally as Lieutenant Governor.

Another memorial to a Racine native is sited at the lake front: NASA astronaut Dr. Laurel Clark, mission specialist, died when the space shuttle *Columbia*, STS-107, was completely destroyed after disintegrating in the atmosphere upon re-entry in 2003.

Racine has the largest Danish settlement in North America. The city has become known for its Danish pastries, particularly the "Kringle," which is crafted in a flat, oval, racetrack-type shape, and made of many feather-light layers of Danish pastry dough, alternated with layers of butter, sprinkled with cinnamon, and filled with a variety of either pecans, almonds paste, cheese, or a fruit filling—yummy! Racine has many Danish bakeries. Over the years, there have been many letters-to-the-editor in the local newspaper (*Racine Journal Times*) about the "Kringle wars." My family members frequented O&H Bakery and Larsen Bakery.

MANUFACTURING TOWN

Why has Racine been referred to as "Invention City"? For many years, Racine has been a traditional blue-collar manufacturing town with production started in the mid-1800s:

- J.I Case Co. manufactured wheat threshing machines and steam engines for farmers. Later, it produced farm tractors and construction equipment. Today, after several mergers, the company name is CNH Global.

- Mitchell Wagon Co. manufactured covered wooden wagons for long journeys, and open wagons for farm use. The company later manufactured motorcycles and automobiles and changed its name to Mitchell Motor Co.

- Rev. James Carhart, considered the "Father of the Automobile," built the first self-propelled, two-cylinder steam engine-driven highway vehicle named Spark.

- Johnson Wax Co. started by manufacturing parquet wooden flooring. Then it developed wax products to help preserve its floors. The wax was derived from carnauba palm trees in South America. The company later offered household cleaning, personal care, and insect control products. The company has changed its name to S.C. Johnson Co., and remains a privately held, family company.

- William Horlick invented malted milk powder, which is a mixture of dried whole milk with extracts of wheat and malted barley.

- The Belle City Manufacturing Company was founded in 1882 following a merger between the David Lawton Company and Racine Brake Company and made farm machinery. The company went out of business around 1948.

In the early 1900s, more companies started up:

- Western Printing & Lithography Co. was established for publishing children's books, Golden Books Encyclopedia, boxed games, jigsaw puzzles, maps, playing cards, stationery, greeting cards, cookbooks, and board games. Over the years, after a series of mergers and company changes, the company name changed to Golden Books Family Entertainment, and was acquired by Penguin Random House.

- Walker Manufacturing Co. made springs, jacks and automotive parts.

- Reliance Controls Co. produced commercial time switches, clocks and electronic controls.

- Hamilton Beach Co. manufactured small electric motors, and later, many home kitchen consumer appliances.

- Modine Manufacturing Co., a thermal management company, designed radiators for cars and tractors.

- Twin Disc Co. made clutches for farm tractors.

- Young Radiator Co. manufactured radiators for trucks and military vehicles.

- Dremel Co. produced small power tools for home and hobby applications.

- InSinkErator Co. developed food waste disposers for kitchen sinks, and later, offered instant hot water dispensers.

- Haban Manufacturing Co. developed a corn "husking-shelling" machine, and later, produced lawn mowers and snow blowers.

Pro Sports

In 1943, the All-American Girls Professional Baseball League was started because of the lack of men that were serving in WWII. It began with four teams—the Racine team was called the "Belles." The team was well supported in the community. The league later expanded to 10 teams throughout the Midwest. The league lasted for 11 years, ending in 1954. It is commemorated in the movie, *A League of Their Own.*

Racine has had a semi-professional football team, the Raiders, since 1953. The team is part of the Mid-States

Football League, and is the oldest minor league football team still operating in Wisconsin. They have received a total of nine national titles. The organization is composed entirely of volunteers. I volunteered many times at practices and at games.

CHANGES

Racine has seen several significant changes since my school days.

GAS WORKS AND NATURAL GAS

Starting in the mid-1800s, a gas works supplied town gas for street lighting and commercial space heating. The gas is a flammable mixture containing carbon monoxide, carbon dioxide, hydrogen, and methane, generated from steam-pyrolysis of coal. I remember seeing huge piles of coal along the lake front and along the Root River, and two huge gas holders. The gas holders were large vertical, cylindrical, open metal-lattice structures that stored the gas under an internal floating roof that was sealed with a flexible curtain around its perimeter.

At the time, coal was also a major fuel for home heating. Interestingly, coal had to be shipped across the Great Lakes from Ohio, as coal is NOT a natural resource to Wisconsin. Then, in the mid-1950s, distributed natural gas replaced town gas. The gas works were shut-down and the gas holders were removed. Natural gas was piped in from several other states, since it is also NOT a natural resource to Wisconsin.

MANUFACTURING EMPLOYMENT

In the 1970s, the Federal Government opened trading relations with China. That turned out to be a huge financial benefit for U.S. manufacturers, who started "offshoring" labor intensive jobs to China. China offered an efficient and cheaper workforce, as well as lower raw material costs. The results were lower product prices for U.S. consumers. Unfortunately, many companies in Racine shut down labor-intensive operations, and greatly reduced employment. Many old manufacturing buildings have been demolished. The city population has decreased as well, from over 90,000 when I was in high school, to about 78,000 today.

LAKE MICHIGAN FISHING

The traffic of ocean ships from all over the world allowed the invasion of several marine creatures, alewives, sea lamprey (eels), and zebra muscles. In the summer, alewives, (small fish less than 10 inches in length) would die off by the tons and float up onto the beaches. Tremendous stench!

Sea Lamprey decimated the lake trout and other fish populations. Overfishing almost eliminated whitefish, herring, yellow perch, and smelt. Fortunately, when I was in high school, the DNR instituted regulations to limit commercial fishing. The DNR then employed selective poisons to control the sea lamprey population. To combat the alewives, DNR began stocking predatory game fish, like chinook salmon, coho salmon and lake trout. The result has been a tremendous success for Lake Michigan. Recreational and sport fishing has expanded greatly, except for yellow perch and smelt. Racine hosts a popular week-long, annual fishing tournament and festival called the "Salmon-A-Rama."

MARINA

Racine always had a protected harbor at the mouth of the Root River. North and south piers jutted far out into the lake. However, with the tremendous success of recreational and sport fishing, a huge marina, now filled with expensive motor boats and sailboats, occupies the harbor.

CONSUMER SHOPPING

During my school years, up through high school, downtown Racine had a bustling Main Street that featured a Woolworth's Five & Dime store, department stores, specialty clothing stores, pharmacies, restaurants, taverns, jewelry stores, furniture stores, banks and two movie theaters. Then Regency Mall was built near the outskirts of town. Main Street almost became a ghost town, but it is surviving today by trying to re-invent itself. In the last few years, on-line shopping with direct shipping to consumers has also greatly changed consumer habits.

THE RACINE ZOO

Racine has had a family-friendly, 28-acre, FREE zoo along the lake front for many years. Free parking has always been available. However, in 2007, economics forced the management to start charging a small entrance fee. It is still a great place for a family outing.

BICYCLE TRAILS

Around the year 2000, the city designed two sets of paved bicycling/walking trails. The Lake Michigan Pathway extends about ten miles along the lakeshore. The Root River Pathway extends about four miles west from the lake. These wonderful trails both connect to other regional trails. I have enjoyed riding and walking them many times.

STONE QUARRIES

Racine had four large, very deep commercial stone quarries—two are still active. These quarries supplied the rock to build the two piers for the lake harbor, and the artificial breakwater barriers to protect much of the shoreline from erosion. Crushed stone continues to be used to build roads and highways around the region. One quarry filled with water and is used for quenching by a heat-treating company. Another quarry, adjacent to the Root River, filled with water and has been turned into a 40-acre county park: Quarry Lake Park. The lake covers about 18 acres. It was a great swimming hole for me.

RIVER BEND NATURE CENTER

River Bend Nature Center was established after I graduated from high school. I did not visit there until many years later when my adopted dad told me it was a great place to go hiking and enjoy the fundraiser events. The Center occupies about 80 acres of woods and wetlands along the Root River. It offers two ponds, many hiking trails, kids' environmental education camps, kayak/canoe outings and springtime "sugaring-off" pancake breakfasts, served with real maple syrup.

I volunteered many hours as a hike leader, welcoming guests to the "Sun's Sugarbush"—a group of sugar maple trees. The tour explains how trees put sugar into the sap by utilizing a natural chemical reaction called photosynthesis. Chlorophyll (the green pigment in the leaves), absorbs energy from the sun, and combines carbon dioxide gas absorbed from the air with water absorbed through the underground roots. A secondary, but very important, product of this magical reaction is the evolution of oxygen gas back into the air.

The sap collection and cooking processes to produce maple syrup are also demonstrated. The sugar maple is Wisconsin's state tree.

Near the big pond is a memorial bench seat labelled "In Loving Memory to Clarence 'Charlie' Burt," my adopted dad.

Richard C. Burt

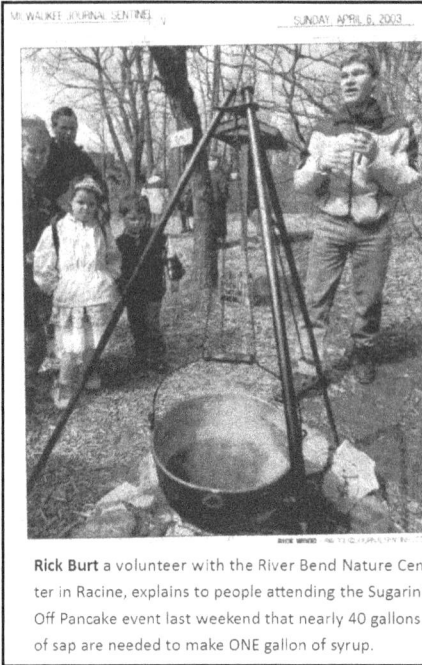

Rick Burt a volunteer with the River Bend Nature Center in Racine, explains to people attending the Sugarin' Off Pancake event last weekend that nearly 40 gallons of sap are needed to make ONE gallon of syrup.

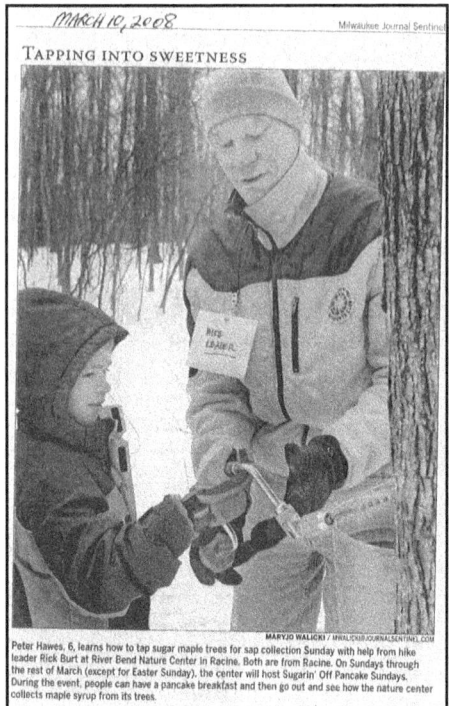

MARCH 10, 2008   Milwaukee Journal Sentinel

TAPPING INTO SWEETNESS

MARYJO WALICKI / MWALICKI@JOURNALSENTINEL.COM

Peter Hawes, 6, learns how to tap sugar maple trees for sap collection Sunday with help from hike leader Rick Burt at River Bend Nature Center in Racine. Both are from Racine. On Sundays through the rest of March (except for Easter Sunday), the center will host Sugarin' Off Pancake Sundays. During the event, people can have a pancake breakfast and then go out and see how the nature center collects maple syrup from its trees.

Chapter 3
CHANGING FAMILIES

I WAS BORN INTO A POOR FAMILY of eight kids: three boys and five girls. I was the second youngest. Jackie was the oldest—14 years my senior. Marlene was 11 years older than me. Judy was ten years older than me. Ron was eight years older (exactly) than me. Kathy was six years older than me. Allen was three years older than me. Finally, Janet was the baby, one year behind me. We lived in a residential neighborhood of Racine, in a house with two floors, stairsteps inside the house, and an external set of stairs on the side the house.

I have only a few memories of my very early years together with my siblings. One, when I was in an upstairs bedroom, sitting on a bed and playing with toys. I stored the toys in a hole in the wall near the bed. My brothers Ron (whom I called Butchie—why?) and Allen were throwing darts (or something) at a target drawn on one wall.

Another time, I was outside, across the street, pulling around a wagon — Janet was sitting in the wagon. We were watching older kids play in the school yard. Then, Janet and I were sitting in the wagon, outside a small neighborhood convenient store a few blocks from our house. We were watching a man unload soda bottles from a truck and taking them into the store. Many years later, I would learn from my older sister Kathy the real reason we were at the store.

In later years' discussions with my siblings, we always referred to our biological parents as Mother and Father. I have learned much of our early life from my brother Ron, and in the past few years from my elder sisters. When they married, Mother was 19, Father was 38 years old. Mother was *somewhat* of a homemaker, never worked outside the home, suffered from seizure attacks (undiagnosed) her entire life, and as you can imagine, was pregnant most of the time.

Mother was the daughter of German immigrants, and had one brother—my Uncle Frederick. My German grandparents lived on the same street, a few blocks away. Uncle Frederick lived with my grandparents. Father worked at the J.I. Case tractor factory, a large area employer. Father was the son of English immigrants. I have no memory of my English grandparents. My personal memories of Mother are very limited — no memory of Father; However, I have two photographs of our biological family: 1) Mother, Grandma and eight children (me at four years old, not Father) and 2) Sister Janet and Me same day.

Father had a close friend from work. That family lived on the other side of town, and had four girls—one named Rose, a year older than me. Our family would sometimes visit them to pick-up garden vegetables to feed

Biological Family

Top row: Grandma, Marlene, Judy, Mother & Jackie

Second row: Kathy & Butchie (Ron)

Bottom row: Allen (Tom), Rick (4 years old) & Janet

Rick (age 4) and sister Janet

our large family. The family connections would continue into the future.

FIRST THAT DAY

I was about three years old (no written records to my knowledge) when one day, a strange lady walked through the front door. Mother told me to go with the lady to stay with some other people for a while. I did not question why—ok with me, no emotion. (Over the years, I have wondered why I didn't feel any emotion. I should have naturally cried to stay home with Mother and my biological family.) I do not remember anyone else being in the house.

The lady was from County Social Services. We walked out of the house and she helped me into a car. I remember it was a warm (summer?) day. In the car, I was so short that I could see only the blue sky and trees. After a long ride out of the city, the car stopped in a driveway at a house out in the Racine countryside. The lady driver opened my car door and I saw green grass in front of me. Now, I had, of course, seen grass before, but not a large yard like this. Then, I noticed the house, where a man and a woman were sitting on the front porch steps. The lady driver picked me up out of the car, set me on the ground, and helped me walk to the house. The man and woman stood up. The woman then picked me up and gave me a huge hug. These would be my foster parents (Mom and Dad), and this would be my new home in a residential community called Crestview. After talking a few minutes, the lady driver left—I never saw her again. That is all that I remember of THAT DAY.

The next morning, I walked into the kitchen thinking of breakfast. The woman (my future Mom) greeted me and asked me what I would like for breakfast. I said that I always had cereal. She then opened a cabinet door, and pulled out three boxes of cereal.

"Which kind do you want?" she asked.

I said that I always had that one, as I pointed to one box. She then walked across the kitchen to the refrigerator, and grabbed a bottle of milk. She then poured cereal into a bowl and started to pour the milk on top of my cereal.

I stopped her. "What are you doing?" I asked.

She had a surprised look on her face, and asked me, "Don't you want milk on your cereal?" I said that I always had water on my cereal. I noticed tears on the woman's face.

"Did I say something wrong?" I asked.

She said, "No, but today you are going to have milk and sugar on your cereal." That was ok with me.

Over the next few days, I wondered where my brothers and sisters were. However, I did not ask. I thought about Grandma—no thoughts of Mother or Father. I felt a deep affection for Grandma, but no love from or for Mother or Father. I realized that my life was much better in this new home—I was now a lucky kid. I would now be raised as an only child by two *loving* foster parents. Had my siblings also gone to foster homes? And, more importantly, what happened, and why? My foster parents offered no information.

Over the years, I learned from my biological siblings what happened. Apparently, after eight children, alcohol abuse, adultery, lack of money, and the large differential in their ages, Mother and Father started arguing a lot and decided to divorce. Had they had eight children out of love for raising children OR simply as a result of frequent pregnancies?

Father moved out to an apartment. Mother stayed in the house with us kids and collected welfare payments. Mother had an offer for marriage from another man. However, he did not want to deal with eight children. Soooo, Mother decided to give up her children for a re-marriage. (Had it been a tough decision?). Mother would soon give birth to another child, our step-sister, Joy— whom I never met. Many years later, I learned that Mother died at age 38, shortly after Joy was born.

GRANDMA VISITS

I would be allowed to visit Grandma three times. One day, several months later, that December, the telephone rang. My foster Mom answered, and talked a long while, then hung up. She called me into the kitchen. She said, "That was your sister Jackie. She wants you to go to your Grandma's for a Christmas Eve family gathering."

I was surprised and confused. I had not heard anything from my biological family. Mom then said, "We had plans to go to Waukesha to visit your new aunt, uncle, and cousins. What do you want to do?"

I thought that was a tough, unfair question to pose to a three-year-old foster kid who had not seen his siblings or grandmother for several months!

Of course, I shouted, "I want to go to Grandma's!"

Mom was disappointed at my response. However, she agreed to let me go. My foster Dad drove me to my Grandma's house in the city, and dropped me off, to pick me up later.

At Grandma's house for Christmas, I reunited with my siblings, Grandma and Uncle Frederick—lots of hugs and kisses. Everyone except my sister Marlene was there. Grandpa was sitting quietly in his rocking chair, not talking or moving, just staring ahead. I climbed up onto his lap and hugged him, but he did not respond.

Then, Grandma picked me up and said that Grandpa was not feeling well. He apparently had dementia. I noticed that my oldest sister, Jackie, was tall and had dark hair—the rest of us had blonde hair.

In the kitchen was a large gingerbread house on the table — WOW! The dining room had a long table set up for a lot of people to eat. A large crystal chandelier hung above the table.

After dinner, we all gathered in the living room. Janet and I were sitting on the floor. Presents were passed around. Jackie seemed to be the coordinator. I was overwhelmed at all the gifts that I got. I wanted to save all the pretty wrapping paper with the ribbons and bows, along with my gifts (apparently, that was the root of my natural inclination for recycling and environmental conservation). Everyone laughed at me, and said not to save the wrapping paper, but that I could save the ribbons and bows. When I got home, I showed my foster mom my collection of ribbons and bows.

During the middle of the gift exchanges, Grandma picked me up and carried me out of the living room to a bedroom. She said that there was someone who wanted to meet me. I was confused. After walking into the bedroom, the door swung open slightly away from the wall. A tall, slender, dark-haired lady was standing in the corner. Grandma handed me to the lady.

"Do you know who this is?" asked Grandma.

I had no clue and said, "No.". The lady gave me a kiss and a big hug for a few seconds. Neither of them said anything else. The lady handed me back to Grandma, and we walked back to the living room. *Who was that?* I wondered, but I did not ask anyone. Why was that lady hiding in the bedroom? To this day, no one has been able to confirm who the lady was, but she must have been Mother.

The second time I visited Grandma was during my sister Jackie's wedding, I think in the springtime. I do not remember who else was there. Several of us went up into the attic. There was a large, old, wooden cabinet with a big bell-shaped horn sticking out of the top. It was called a Victrola phonograph player. Someone picked me up to look inside the top of the cabinet. I saw a circular table inside with a large arm from one side with a needle at one end. I was told that the arm needle played records for music.

Then we looked through a small collection of thick, heavy, circular, vinyl records. Someone placed one record on the cabinet table and turned a hand crank on the side of the cabinet. We heard orchestra music, no singing. I always wondered what happened to that old Victrola—it was probably a valuable antique. Many years later, I learned that my sister Jackie inherited it, and then passed it on to one of her sons.

Then Uncle Frederick took me down in the basement. A large pile of coal had been place by one wall. He explained how a truck delivered the coal down a chute through the window. He picked up a large chunk and let me touch it — it was black, hard, and somewhat shiny, and made my finger black. He said that the coal was burned in the furnace for room heating.

Finally, I remember everyone walking out of Grandma's house, cheering and throwing things (rice?) into the air as Jackie and her new husband, Gil, got into a car and drove away.

The third time I visited Grandma, several months later, my foster Mom came with me. While Mom and Grandma talked in the kitchen, I helped Uncle Frederick hang a picture on the wall. I have no idea what they talked about—probably family issues. Uncle Frederick then took me down in the basement. No coal pile this time. They had a new gas-fired furnace. We had lunch. That was the last time that I saw Grandma, but I would see Uncle Frederick again. I was four years old.

Chapter 4
CRESTVIEW SUBDIVISION

LAMBERTON FARMS WERE LOCATED on the Lake Michigan shoreline about five miles north of Racine. Two adjacent family farms occupied about 400 acres. I will present my thoughts of how the farms became my foster home community, with the help of three articles from the *Racine Journal Times*:

- "Crestview School Addition", Oct. 22, 1959
- "Crestview had Quiet Past", June 29, 1975
- "Welcome to Crestview", July 11, 1998

In the mid-1800s, when the Racine area was being settled by European immigrants, a Bohemian family cleared the land, and started farming. Wheat was the initial crop; but they later expanded to strawberries, cabbage, sugar beets and dairy cows.

A southern area of the farms had a deposit of sand and gravel. The family mined the deposit to supply construction material for local highways. Much of the sand and gravel was also shipped by barges to Chicago. Remnants of an old dirt, gravel road down the side of the lake bluff, and concrete silos on the beach, are still visible today. The farms and the surrounding communities thrived until about 1916.

During the First World War, the government purchased almost all of Lamberton and began construction of a huge TNT manufacturing facility. The war ended in 1918, before the plant was finished and operational. Eventually, the land was returned to local control. Then, after World War Two, the farmland was purchased by a Chicago real estate developer, Abner Rosenfeld.

Rosenfeld built about a dozen two-bedroom summer resort cottages for his "Jewish Intellectual" friends, and called the community Crestview. The cottages were all wood construction, each of unique design, and some with names. As the community grew, modern, three-bedroom modest houses with basements were built. The community roads were all dirt and some gravel, with unique names: Lamberton Road (the main entrance to the community), Paul Bunyan Road (where I grew up), Lakeshore Drive (along the lake), Cliffside Drive, Indian Trail, Blackhawk Drive, Sunrise Road, Pheasant Trail, and Arrowhead Street.

In the summer, road dust was in the air whenever a vehicle passed by our house. Once a year, a county road crew would spray an oil /tar mixture on the roads for dust control. For several days after, we had to walk only on the sides of the roads to avoid the sticky road surface. Over the years, most of the roads were surfaced with rough asphalt.

The Crestview subdivision had about 100 houses when I was a kid. The entire east side was the lake bluff — below about 100 feet was a narrow beach and the water surface. On the north and west sides of the community was a large ravine with a small creek at the bottom (usually almost dry) that emptied into the lake. On both sides of the ravine were woods with lots of trees and some old, overgrown farm fields. On the other side of the ravine and woods was an active farm that grew mostly soybeans.

It was almost a Garden of Eden for me, with old apple and pear trees, mulberry trees, crab apple trees, wild strawberries and raspberries, along with the white birch, oak, and maple trees. I frequently saw wild animals, like birds (lots of crows, Canadian geese and seagulls), ring-necked pheasants (a beautiful game bird), cotton-tail Rabbits, an occasional white-tailed deer or red fox, and unfortunately, coyotes and lots of mosquitos.

Along the ravine and the side of the lake bluff was an old dirt and gravel access road down to the beach. The lake bluff was mostly bare dirt and clay soil—lots of erosion onto the beach and into the water during rain storms. The water surface near the shore was frequently very turbid from the erosion. The limited beach was a mixture of sand and rounded rocks. Lake Michigan water is very cold. It was usually late July before the water was warm enough to enjoy swimming. What a great place for a kid to play with the woods, ravine, beach and old farm fields.

In addition, many houses were under construction with large holes being dug out in the ground for basements, leaving huge dirt piles for us kids to play on—great fun!

At the community entrance was a baseball field. I played many hours of practice and organized Little League and Pony League games there.

CRESTVIEW SCHOOL

When I was about five years old, Mr. Rosenfeld donated five acres of land along the ravine for the construction of a school. Lots of trees were cleared away for the building and the playgrounds. Several times, Dad and I drove to the cleared site. There was a huge pile of large trees that had been knocked down. Dad used a chain saw to collect firewood. I played on the pile of trees—great fun!

The school building was constructed of cement blocks with brick facing. It had a flat roof. Initially, the building had only four rooms, but was expanded to eight rooms in later years. The school was funded through local community property taxes. Grades one through eight were supported — there was no kindergarten. Dad served on the local school board.

When I was 11 years old (fifth grade), the school board voted to join the Racine Unified School District and to abandon our local school. The decision was controversial among the community. It greatly reduced local property taxes, though now little kids would have to catch a school bus to Racine.

I completed sixth grade in the Crestview School, then started taking a school bus into Racine for junior high and high school. The old school building has since been converted into a community Catholic church.

SAND PITS

On the south side of the community was a large farm that grew cabbage and potatoes and surrounded several acres of land that we called the "Sand Pits." It had several large dugout holes filled with water and mounds of sand hills. In the summer, we kids would ride our bikes up and down the hills, and catch frogs in the ponds. In the winter, we ice skated on the frozen ponds. It was a great place to play!

I always wondered about some sort of connection between the sand pits and the old dirt and gravel road down the side of the lake bluff, and the concrete silos on the beach. I would not learn of the connection until the newspaper articles many years later.

Today, the Crestview Subdivision has greatly expanded to about 1,200 houses, taking over adjacent farmland, and covering the old sand pits. That made me a little sad many years later when I noticed the changes. I mentioned to Dad that I hoped that the sand pits would have been preserved as a park for kids to play at.

Dad responded, "I guess no one thought of that."

There might still be a few rabbits in the nearby woods. However, coyotes and over-hunting have eliminated the pheasant and red fox populations. One positive change in wildlife is the recent occurrence of bald eagles in the area. In a few places, bluff erosion has been somewhat reduced by placement of large rocks. However, between the ravine and the adjacent farm fields, the bluff has receded greatly.

Most community residents are in the middle income bracket: truck drivers, carpenters, electricians, and factory workers. The community entrance now has a convenient store, deli, hair salon and gas station—the old baseball field is gone. However, the west side of the old farmland has been converted to a county park with several baseball fields, Cliffside Park. Only a few of the adjacent farms still exist, growing soybeans, cabbage, potatoes, and strawberries.

Chapter 5
ADOPTION

WHEN I WAS FOUR YEARS OLD, I had been living with my foster parents for about a year. One evening at the dinner table, Mom and Dad told me that they loved me very much and that they wanted to adopt me. I did not know exactly what they meant. I felt comfortable and happy being raised as an only child, even though I missed my biological siblings.

Mom explained that if they adopted me, then NO ONE could take me away from them. *Why would someone take me away from them?* I thought. I noticed tears in Mom's eyes. I looked at Dad—he had an unusually sad facial expression.

"OK with me," I said.

They both smiled. Mom then explained that tomorrow we would go to the county courthouse to visit a judge to make it legal. I did not understand until many years later *three* critical things: 1) County Social Services monitor foster care; 2) Mom was not biologically able to birth children; and 3) Mom was actually much older than she listed on the adoption papers.

SECOND THAT DAY

The Racine County Courthouse is a large, tall concrete building. Mom, Dad, and I took an elevator up many floors. We then entered the judge's chambers. Mom sat in a chair, picked me up on her lap, wrapped her arms around me, and held me tight. After they talked a few minutes, the judge asked me to sit on HIS lap. He then asked me if I wanted the Burts to adopt me.

I said, "Yes."

The judge then told me to walk out into the hallway and sit on the bench seat and wait while he talked with Mom and Dad. After a few minutes, they all walked out of the office and over to me. Mom picked me up and cried, "You now belong to us —no one can take you away."

After the adoption, Mom requested that the State Board of Health "amend" (defined as, "to change or modify for the better—to alter formally") my birth certificate, and to destroy my original document. My last name was changed. My parents' names are now listed as my new Mom and Dad. The ages of my new parents are now listed as Dad at 30; Mom at 34.

I learned many years later that Mom was actually 41. She was concerned that her real age would complicate the adoption process. I actually never looked at my birth certificate until many years later—why should I? Once I inspected the document, I noticed that the place of my birth (hospital, home) is not listed, except to be in Racine.

The document no longer shows my biological last name, or my biological parents' names.

I did not realize the importance of THAT DAY until many years later, but I did feel happy—I was a lucky kid! My life path was much brighter than could have been possible had I not been adopted. How did I manage to connect with these two loving people?

AFTER THE WAR

Mom and Dad had both served in the Army Air Force during World War Two, Mom as a nurse, Dad as a mechanic and test pilot in the motor pool. They met while stationed in Puerto Rico. Mom had seen Dad a few times around the military base. She thought that she would like to meet him. So, one day she walked over to the hangar where she thought Dad was working. She asked around where she might find Charlie Burt. She was told that he was lying under an airplane nearby.

Mom noticed his feet sticking out from under the plane. So, she walked over by him, and kicked his feet. Dad yelled out, "Who is kicking my feet?" He then crawled out from under the plane. Mom then said, "Oh, I am sorry, I just tripped over your feet". They were married upon discharge from the Army.

In Chapter 3, I mentioned a family with four daughters—one named Rose—who was very friendly with my biological family. An interesting coincidence is that Rose's father served in the Army Air Force during World War Two at Puerto Rico, in the same hangar as my new

Dad. The connections between Rose and me would grow much stronger over the years.

They then moved to Tulsa, Oklahoma, and operated a small store and gas service station for about six years. Dad got frustrated with the lack of business and poor income, and decided to leave by himself to go to Milwaukee, Wisconsin to find a better job. He immediately found a good-paying job at a small engine manufacturer. About a year later, Mom joined him in Wisconsin. A year after that, they visited Crestview, moved into one of the two-bedroom summer cottages, and took out a 12-year mortgage.

NEW MOM

Mom was born in Kansas, but raised in Oklahoma. She had three sisters and one brother. Mom stayed home with me and took care of the house. She missed not having a little girl to care for. So, she became a volunteer Girl Scout leader. I had to stay in my room while the girls were in the house for their meetings.

Mom also enjoyed politics. She volunteered at the county polls during every election. She was also active in the community and with the PTA. Mom was well-liked in the community, but she could be a real "bear" on days that she did not feel well.

Mom had a really variable "Dr. Jekyll and Mr. Hyde"-type personality. She liked to tease me and the neighborhood kids. Mom enjoyed referring (affectionately) to me as her "Little Monkey," because I had bowed legs and big ears. When Mom did not feel well, she would lecture me. She would sit on the living room couch, and I would stand across the room with my arms folded. She would tell me that I was a cold-hearted, unthankful, rotten kid — she never should have taken me in from *that* family. I listened, but I sensed something was wrong, because Mom was so loving on her "good" days. The lectures continued in car rides during shopping trips, and in letters to me when I was away at college.

Mom was never happy on holidays: Christmas, her birthday, and Mother's Day. She always cried and complained when she did not get the gifts that she liked. I felt sorry for Dad—he had NO CLUE what gifts to give Mom, or how to make her happy, but he tried his best.

Mom had frequent health problems. Every winter, she contracted colds and the flu. Mom was a heavy smoker. I think that was a major contributor. After dinner, Mom and Dad would talk current events and politics, drink coffee, and smoke cigarettes.

I would ask to be excused from the table so that I would not have to breathe in the smoke. I thought smoking was a disgusting habit! Several times, Mom blew smoke in my face and said, "It will not hurt you!" I guess that she, and everyone, in those days believed that smoking or second-hand smoke were NOT harmful—the tobacco industry did a masterful marketing job for their products. I suggested to Mom that cigarette smoking may not be healthy, and that she should quit. She told me that she enjoyed smoking, and for me to mind my own business.

NEW DAD

Dad was born and raised in Antigo, Wisconsin. He had three sisters. After high school, Dad served about a year as a fire lookout for the Civilian Conservation Corps (CCC). After moving to Crestview, Dad worked in Kenosha as a tool-and-die maker for a large automotive manufacturer, American Motors Company. The cars they made were called Ramblers. Local people referred to them a "Kenosha Cadillacs."

We owned several Ramblers over the years, because Dad got a 20 percent employee discount. Ramblers were inexpensive (read as cheaply made) cars, designed as an alternative to compete with GMC, Ford, and Chrysler. Our cars were a maintenance headache. Dad was always trying to repair them.

Dad commuted the ten miles to work in a carpool with several other neighborhood men. One cold, snowy, winter day, it was Dad's turn to drive and pick up the other men. Unfortunately, they never made it to work that day—one front wheel fell off the car! Dad usually had a mild, even personality, but that day he was NOT happy!

Dad was also active and well-liked in the community. He served on the local school board, and coached the Little League baseball team for many years. Dad had a very friendly personality—he did lots of favors for our neighbors. He also liked to tease me and the neighborhood kids. Dad never got sick—he seemed to be always healthy, even when Mom and I got sick.

However, Dad did suffer from some ailments. Many times, he would come home from work complaining of backaches and headaches. He showed me how to help him. He sometimes would lie down on the living room couch and taught me how to rub his forehead and temples to relieve his headaches. Other days, he would lie on the living room floor (carpeted), face down, and I would walk barefoot up and down his back.

When I was in high school, he had an asthma attack, and spent a day in the hospital. Dad was also a heavy smoker. However, I convinced him to quit for a few years.

Dad and I were grouse hunting one day walking through a woods. He surprisingly suggested that we stop and rest for a while.

"Why?" I asked.

He said he needed to catch his breath. As we sat on a large log, Dad pulled out a pack of cigarettes and lit up. I always hated the fact that Mom and Dad smoked. Something came over me.

I looked at Dad, and asked him, "Do you think that smoking cigarettes could contribute to your breathing problems?"

As soon as I finished my question, I thought, "I am dead! Dad is going to smack me!" I was always very respectful toward Dad—I had never before talked back to him.

45

Dad looked at me, then looked at the cigarette, took one more puff, and then threw the butt on the ground, and smashed it out with his foot.

He then said, "You are right—I quit!" And, he did quit smoking for about 20 years, until Mom got heart problems.

Many years later, I once asked Dad when he had started smoking. Had he started in high school? He said that he did not start smoking until he was in the military— no money to buy cigarettes while in high school. The tobacco companies supplied FREE cigarettes for all military personnel. The tobacco companies knew that nicotine was addictive—a great marketing idea.

Dad was my mentor. He taught me how to fish; how to hunt; how to trap shoot; how to catch and throw a baseball and football; how to tend a garden; and how to do maintenance on the house, the yard, and our cars. We enjoyed many hours together watching sports on television: Green Bay Packers football, Milwaukee Braves and Brewers baseball, and Milwaukee Bucks basketball. He especially enjoyed watching hockey on TV. About once a year, we would go to Milwaukee County Stadium to watch a baseball or football game. The Packers played one game a year in Milwaukee.

Dad planted a garden every spring in the backyard. We grew strawberries, lettuce, radishes, tomatoes, cucumbers, sweet corn, and green peppers. He planted marigold flowers around the perimeter to try to deter rabbits. I enjoyed the natural foods, though I did not enjoy my chores of weeding and watering the garden. We shared much of the harvest with our neighbors. Dad also made a triangular wooden compost bin with one side as a hinged door. We composted food scraps, grass clippings, hedge cuttings, and tree leaves—great fertilizer for the garden.

Dad liked to play card games. He taught me how to play cribbage and Schafkopf (aka, Sheepshead) - the German (Bavarian) card game that is very popular in Wisconsin.

Dad was also somewhat of a multi-tasker. He enjoyed the challenge of assembling jig-saw puzzles while listening to a sports broadcast on his transistor radio (usually through an ear connection). He also liked to play the self-card game Solitaire while listening to a sports broadcast. In fall, he was really in his element. He would tune the television to a football game, listen to a baseball playoff or World Series game with the transistor radio plugged into one ear, while reading a newspaper or magazine.

NEW RELATIVES

I learned about my Mom and Dad's sides of the new family. In Waukesha, just west of Milwaukee, lived one of Dad's sisters and her husband—Aunt Louise and Uncle Erv, with their two children, my new cousins, Bobby and Tari. We visited them frequently. I met Dad's other sisters only once. Dad's father, Grandpa Burt, lived in Antigo. We visited him every summer during vacation trips.

Mom had a sister in Tulsa, Oklahoma—Aunt Myrtle —and Aunt Hazel in Little Rock, Arkansas. I met each of them once.

When I was about five years old, I had a light green octopus doll. I asked all my new relatives, and some friends, to sign their names on a leg of the doll. *Whatever happened to that doll?* I wonder.

NEW HOUSE

Our house in Crestview was one of the unique, original two-bedroom summer cottages. It was less than 1,000 square feet. Mr. Rosenfeld named it "The Lighthouse." The living room had a high ceiling with a horizontal row of square windows at the top, on two sides, just below the pitched roof line. It also had large, floor-to-ceiling windows at three corners.

The house had no insulation. Redwood siding covered two sides of the exterior and two walls inside the living room. The rest of the house had a flat roof over bedrooms, the kitchen, and a utility room. For winter warmth, there were two oil-fired floor heaters set in the crawl space under the house: One was located in the hallway to the bedrooms and one was between the kitchen and the living room. Keeping comfortable and warm those first few winters was a challenge.

The driveway was grass and dirt—no car port or garage. The lot was about a quarter of an acre with a nice, large backyard. The front yard had two tall elm trees and smaller red cedar trees. Lots of grass to cut!

Over the years, as finances allowed, Mom and Dad made many upgrades to the property. They planted a row of hedges on both sides and along the back of the yard. They planted rose bushes and other flowers around the house. The first house revision was to permanently cover up the living room rows of windows near the ceiling for winter warmth. Then, the interior redwood siding was removed from the living room, and insulation installed in the walls with plasterboard sheet walls. Mom hated the redwood siding in the living-room—it was dark and attracted dust.

Next, insulation was installed in the living room ceiling and kitchen ceiling, covering up the exposed wooden beams. The rest of the house remained uninsulated. The oil heaters were removed and replaced with a natural-gas-fired furnace with forced air circulation ductwork.

When I was in high school, we got our first window air conditioner for summer cooling. Eventually, the entire exterior of the house was covered with white aluminum siding. Finally, a two-car garage was built and part of the driveway between the house and garage was cemented. Later on, the remainder of the driveway was covered with asphalt when a road crew surfaced the community roads.

The community water supply was from a local well. Mom complained a lot about the "hard water"—high calcium and iron content made it difficult to launder clothes, and left a film on clear drinking glasses. So, we eventually got a water softener. That solved Mom's problems, but I did not like the saline taste of the softened water. About once a month, we had to drain dirty, black water from the softener, and buy a large bag of rock salt to replenish the softener.

I have left the description of the best house "upgrade" to last. Mom hated the small bathroom, small shower, and lack of a linen closet. She wanted a bathtub. Her prayers were answered one day when some community kids decided to break into Mr. Rosenfeld's personal summer cottage, right on the lake bluff, and set it on fire.

Rosenfeld was in Chicago at the time. Mom called him with the sad news. While on the phone, Mom asked if she could retrieve an undamaged, wooden linen cabinet and the bathtub. That was okay with him. So, Mom, Dad, and I extracted the linen cabinet and bathtub, and installed them in our bathroom. That was a major project!

Dad had to rip out the shower, re-plumb the piping, and move the toilet to where the shower was to make room for the tub. Mom wanted to put the linen cabinet in the old shower space, above the toilet. So, we measured the width of the cabinet, and it was exactly the same as the old shower space—no clearance. I told Mom that it would not fit. Mom said we were going to make it fit! With crow bars and much pushing and shoving, the two side walls gave way just enough for the cabinet to slide in. Whew, what an effort! Mom was happy with the results.

MY TWO BROTHERS

Mom and Dad thought that it would be good for me if they also fostered my two older brothers. I liked the idea. So, after they adopted me, Mom and Dad invited my two brothers to live with us. I think I was maybe five or six years old. Ron (Butchie) was 13 or 14 and Allen was eight or nine. They lived with us for only a few months. Here is a memorable photo of Dad, Ron (Butchie), our dog Jiggers, and me.

Dad, Butchie (Ron), Jiggers & Rick (4 years old)

I was in heaven with my big brothers. The three of us shared one bedroom with bunkbeds. Mom said that she loved both of them, and wanted to adopt them. However, Ron and Allen could not adjust to my new parents' lifestyle.

One morning, as I walked through the living room toward the kitchen for breakfast, I saw Ron and Mom yelling at each other—a heated argument. Ron was standing near the kitchen table, holding a glass of milk; Mom was at the other end of the kitchen. I then saw Ron slam down the glass of milk on the table—milk sprayed all over. Mom then slapped Ron across the face.

I did not know the reason for the argument until Ron tried to explain to me when I was older. Apparently, the fight was over ME! I must have misbehaved, and Mom had yelled (excessively?) at me. Ron thought that Mom was being too harsh with me—he wanted to protect his little brother. Ron told Mom to stop yelling at me.

Mom then yelled back at Ron. "Mind your own business. He is my son now."

After the argument, Ron and Allen ran away—I had no idea where they went. I did not see either of them for a long while. I was on my own again.

Chapter 6
BIOLOGICAL FAMILY

SO, WHAT HAPPENED TO MY BIOLOGICAL family while I
was growing up as an only child in Crestview? I knew that
I had two older brothers and five sisters. There was about
a 15-year difference between the oldest and youngest
sibling. I had some contact with a few of my biological
siblings, but no contact for a long time with others. The
following is a combination of my memories, and what I
learned many years later from my surviving siblings (four
have passed away).

One difficulty in this emotional journey was the
necessity to merge conflicting memories. If one did not
personally see or experience something, then did IT
occur? This process has been similar to what scientists
experience during "peer review" of journal articles. I think
that all humans suffer from what is referred to as
"selective memory." It may be much easier to remember
the "good times" rather than the "sad times."

SISTER JACKIE

Jackie was the oldest. She was 17 years old on THAT
DAY for me (I was three years old). She was not fostered

out. She stayed home with Mother for a while, then lived with Grandma and Uncle Frederick when Mother re-married. Jackie did not finish high school, but soon married. My sisters Marlene and Judy served in her wedding.

I do not remember how I found out, but about a year after Jackie married, she gave birth to her first son—I was an uncle, but no contact.

Then, when I was eight years old, one day the phone rang. Mom talked a while, then hung up. She said that was my sister Jackie. Grandpa had died. I was sad, but I had only a slight memory of him.

When I was 14, the phone rang again. Mom talked a while, then hung up. She told me that it was Jackie and that Grandma had died. I was sad, and missed seeing Grandma. Mom liked my grandma—we attended the funeral.

When I was 15, the phone rang again. Mom talked a while, then hung up. She said it was my sister Jackie. My sister Judy had died at age 25. What a shock! No further details (see section on Sister Judy). Mom liked Judy; we attended the funeral. Jackie maintained a close relation-ship with Father. I had no direct contact with Jackie for many years. I learned later that she divorced her first husband, lived with our sister Marlene for a while, then re-married and raised six children.

SISTER MARLENE

Marlene was the second oldest. She was 14 years old when THAT DAY occurred for her. Marlene came home from school to find a social worker in the house waiting for her. The house was empty. Mother was not there. Marlene was confused as to why the social worker was there. (Why would a mother NOT be home to see her second oldest child taken away by Social Services?).

Marlene was the first of us to be taken away from our family. She was taken to a foster family who owned a bakery on the other side of the city. She felt really alone— a strange family, no money, only a few clothes, and no friends. She was told not to contact anyone of her biological family. She never saw Mother again, until Mother died. Marlene saw our sister Jackie one time — that was to be in Jackie's wedding. Marlene and Jackie were never close; they did not like each other. Marlene did try to contact her a few times over the years.

Her foster parents put Marlene to work in the bakery, but never paid her any wages. The money was put into a savings account for future education. It was not difficult work, and she had some fun doing it. Her foster parents were nice to her; However; the rest of the family was just uncomfortable. The other members of the foster family did not want Marlene in their homes because Marlene was a foster child. She was never adopted.

Marlene was not allowed to celebrate holidays with her foster family. When she was ready to graduate from high school, the welfare services department found out that Marlene had money put aside, and that she had to send it to them—what a surprise to Marlene!

After high school, Marlene got a job at a local hospital. She worked long hours, even holidays. She had to pay her own living expenses, but now she finally had some money. When she was 19, Marlene attended nursing school at Walther Memorial Hospital in Chicago. She received two scholarships for college. While in school, she worked on her days out of class and on holidays. She felt alone. She was not contacted by Mother, sister Jackie, or Grandma. At graduation services, Marlene had no family present to congratulate her, but her classmates were good support. She was just happy to have made it through school.

After graduation, Marlene returned to Racine and stayed with some friends until she could get some money together to get an apartment. She got a job as a private scrub nurse for a local medical doctor. She loved that work, and enjoyed the long hours. Then she ran into our sister Judy. Marlene and Judy got an apartment together. They lived there for a while until Judy met her future husband.

When Judy got married, Marlene had to find a new place to live. By chance, our sister Jackie had recently divorced and was in a bind. Jackie had one son at the time, and was not working. Our biological Father asked Marlene if she could help Jackie. So, they found a house to rent and moved in together. That lasted only a short time. The two sisters did not get along well, and Marlene soon met her first future husband. After Marlene married, she moved to Chicago. After a few years, Marlene divorced, and moved to North Carolina to live with a friend.

Marlene practiced her nursing skills in intensive care, surgery, and in the emergency room (ER) at several hospitals. For a while, she lived in Greensboro, NC. Father called her about Judy's death. Then, Father moved to Greensboro to live with Marlene. She experienced many challenges treating Native Americans injured in fights and by Klu Klux Klansmen (KKK). After several years, Marlene and Father moved back to Wisconsin.

Back in Racine, Marlene became a Nurse Practitioner (NP). Marlene worked in the ER at St. Mary's Hospital and at SC Johnson Company. She talked with the doctor who performed the autopsy on Judy's death and read the death certificate. The cause of death was listed as pneumonia.

Marlene did some world travelling. She visited Africa three times. She was in Kenya for ten days on a medical safari. She visited several hospitals, the "Flying Doctors," and tribal doctors. She saw lots of animals and viewed Mt. Kilimanjaro from a distance. She was at the Mt. Kenya Safari Club and went horseback riding in Mt. Kenya. Most of the people spoke English. The tours were mostly run by subcontinental Indians. The best part was seeing the animals.

She also visited South Africa for about the same amount of time. In Cape Town, she stood where the

Atlantic and Indian oceans meet, but could not tell the difference — the blue waters looked the same. She also visited Johannesburg and Soweto. Local authorities would not let her go out by herself because she was white, and they were afraid something might happen to her. So, a guard with a gun always accompanied her.

Marlene was in Lagos, Nigeria for a month doing health exams for SC Johnson Company. She saw no animals, just LOTS of people. She then went to Benin. When she got off the plane, she thought she had stepped into hell — it was so hot! She had her first taste of bush chicken. She does NOT recommend it, for she found out it was RAT.

Marlene loved animals. In Racine, she volunteered at a rescue shelter for abused large animals. Marlene had always wanted to be a large animal veterinarian, but she was told that vocation was for men only. At one time, she housed seven Beagle dogs and a parrot.

In later years, Marlene, my brother Ron and sister Janet became very close siblings. They shared many dinners and visited with their dogs. I had no contact with Marlene until many years later, when I learned that she had married, raised two children, divorced, and re-married.

Marlene shared with me some memories of our biological family. Father's job did NOT pay him much money, so we were a very poor family. Father always cooked dinner and did the laundry each week. He also made homemade bread each week. Father maintained a vegetable garden each summer. Father also loved to go fishing, and would sometimes take one or two kids with him.

Mother was not a great — or even good — housekeeper. She had seizures as a child and all through her life. Marlene thought the seizures were the result from birth trauma. Mother told Marlene to keep away from her during the seizures. Fridays and Saturdays, both Mother and Father drank alcohol a lot at a nearby neighborhood tavern. However, there was no beer in the house.

Father was 20 years older than Mother. Mother did "flirt and mess around," which made Father very angry. Marlene thought that Mother was lonely and looking for love. So, they argued a lot.

Mother and Father had a problem with love. They separated and later divorced. Marlene was surprised that they had stayed together as long as they did. Father moved out of the house and rented an apartment. Mother never worked and there were no alimony payments—we were on welfare. After all of us kids had been taken away or left home, Mother re-married, and had a daughter, Joy. After Mother died, Joy was put in a foster home.

Marlene explained her mixed feelings about our family life to me. Two times each year, we all went to Grandma's house—summer and Christmas—it was great fun! Grandma served egg salad and ham salad sandwiches, a German sausage-type gelatinous dish with beef and pork, and ginger cookies.

Unfortunately, after the separation, the courts told Grandma NOT to have family get-togethers anymore, because it would be too hard on us kids. Marlene (and I) thought that was wrong. Marlene told me, "As I get older, I forgive Mother for giving us up." She told both my sister Janet and me that she has tried to forget family memories—too sad. We should just try to "let it go!" Well, we all have done that—until I decided to write this book.

Marlene had many fond memories of Father. He babysat with our sister Judy's kids until she died. Then, Father moved to Greensboro, NC to live with Marlene, and babysat with her children. From then on, Father and Marlene lived together off and on, over the years, and maintained a very close relationship. Marlene's children loved him very much. Father was a wonderful, loving grandpa for her children. She cared for him in the last few months before he died.

SISTER JUDY

Judy was the third oldest child. She would have been 13 years old on THAT DAY for me. What happened to Judy on THAT DAY? I do not know. However, after high school, Judy ran into our sisters Marlene and Kathy, separately, and shared her apartment with them when she was single.

Judy visited me several times in Crestview when I was very young. What a joyful, loving sister—very friendly and well-liked by everyone. She liked to tell jokes. Judy was known as "Swivel Hips" because of her walking style. I met her boyfriend (husband?) one time. I learned many years later, that she had married, raised three children (two boys, one girl), and divorced—I had no contact with them. When Judy died at age 25, her ex-husband took custody of the two boys for a while. However, they eventually went to a foster family. The baby girl was adopted.

The cause of Judy's death remains a mystery. Her death certificate reads "pneumonia," but the police detective who investigated her death told my brother Ron that there was some suspicion that she had been assaulted. However, no evidence was ever found.

Judy had been a cocktail waitress at a popular local night club. Our biological father was babysitting her kids that night. When Judy got home, she asked Father to stay with her that night, but he decided to leave. The next morning, a neighbor heard the sounds of crying children and called police. The police found Judy dead. (How does a healthy 25-year-old woman suddenly die from pneumonia?).

Father got very depressed about her death. He called our sister Marlene, who was living in North Carolina at the time, about Judy's death. Father then decided to move to North Carolina to live with Marlene.

BROTHER RON

Ron was the fourth oldest. He was 11 years old on THAT DAY for me. Ron was exactly eight years older than me—we shared the same birth date. I reminded him that I was his birthday present when he was eight years old. When our biological parents divorced, Ron lived with Father for a while. Then, after I was adopted, my new Mom and Dad invited him and Allen to live with us in Crestview.

I called Ron "Butchie"—I do not know why. Mom called him "Ronnie." She said many times how good-looking both he and Allen were. While living with us, I enjoyed watching Butchie comb his fairly long, blonde hair — he had a really "cool" hair style. He spent lots of time in front of the bathroom mirror preparing it every morning. He would neatly comb back both sides of his head, then comb hair across the top, and create a wavy, swirl across the front. I would watch in amazement, and think about my and Allen's "butch" haircuts—almost bald!

Those few months that they lived with me were super! One time, Butchie, Allen, and some friends were planning to go out to walk the neighborhood roads. I asked if I could tag along.

Butchie said, "Okay, but you have to walk several feet behind us."

"Yeah, sure!" I replied. He was so cool. I thought he could walk on water. I really missed Butchie and Allen after they left the Burts house. I had no idea where they went. Many years later, I learned that Butchie had lived off and on with Father in Racine, and roomed some time at the local YMCA.

One day, when I was about seven, the phone rang. Mom talked a while, then hung up. She said it was my brother Ronnie—she was happy to hear from him. He was calling from a noisy, outdoor, public phone booth. Hail was pounding down on the roof. He had gotten an A- in geometry class (10th grade, about 15 years old?).

Once Butchie turned 16 and got his driver's license, he often visited me in Crestview. Mom and Dad always welcomed him. When I was about eight (he was 16), one summer day, he rode in on a dark-green motor-scooter. I was alone at the house—Dad was at work and Mom was shopping.

While Butchie and I were playing catch with a baseball in the front yard, a school kid from my class walked down the road. For some reason, that kid did not like me. He stopped by the house, yelled at me, and called me a "chicken." That surprised me, but I had no inclination to respond.

However, brother Butchie was upset. Ron said that I needed to go "knock his block off!" I had never gotten into a fight—I liked everyone. Ron encouraged me and gently pushed me forward. So, I walked out to the road and confronted the kid. He raised both fists—so I did the same. After dancing around each other for a few seconds, I decided to take a swing at his head. He ducked. Then, with an uppercut, he hit me in the stomach—ouch! That knocked the wind out of me. The kid laughed. Butchie then stepped forward and told the kid to leave. After I recovered my breath, Ron gave me a few quick fighting suggestions for next time.

We then decided to go for a ride on his motor-scooter — no helmets in those days. I was thrilled to be riding with my big brother. When we turned down a side road with loose stones, Butchie lost control of the scooter, and we flipped "ass-over-teakettle" with the scooter landing on top of us. Our clothes were torn. Blood oozed from my arm and one leg. Ron was also scraped badly. However, no broken bones.

Butchie said, "Your mom is going to kill me!"

We got back on the scooter and rode home. Ron cleaned us up and left before Mom got back. I changed clothes: I put on a long-sleeve shirt and pants (I usually wore a T-shirt and shorts). When Mom got home, she questioned why I was wearing those clothes. I just shrugged my shoulders. She pulled up one sleeve and noticed my scrape marks. Then she exclaimed, "Your brother Ronnie has been here, hasn't he?" Again, I just shrugged my shoulders. She never knew what really happened. Whew—what a day that was.

One summer day, several years later, I was maybe 16, Ron (maybe 24) visited me while riding a big BSA motorcycle — way cool! He talked with Mom for a long time while all of us sat on the grass in the front yard. He told lots of stories of his childhood activities, meeting a new girlfriend, and mentioned that he wanted to find out the real cause of our sister Judy's death.

He told us that he never remembered our Mother ever hugging him. Mother and Father visited a neighborhood tavern often. When Ron was young, he would go to the tavern to look for Mother and Father. There was an opening in the bottom of the front door to the tavern. Ron would look through the door opening to see Mother and Father, and other men. One time, someone threw a glass of water in his face. (My sister Marlene thought that Ron just imagined some of his stories.) After Mother divorced and re-married, Ron tried to visit Mother, but her new husband would not let him in the house.

Before leaving that day, Butchie gave me a ride on the motorcycle—no helmets again, but no accidents this time.

Several months later, he visited me again, twice. He was now driving a cool burgundy car. We went to a local bowling alley and bowled a few games. Then we played some pool (billiards). I was thrilled! Another day, Butchie visited me and we played cribbage on the living room coffee table.

Then one sad day, the phone rang. Mom talked a while, then hung up. She called me into the living room, and said, "Your brother Ronnie has been arrested for burglary at a gas service station. He is in jail."

She then told Dad that they needed to go to the county courthouse to post Ronnie's bail. Ron and a friend had decided to steal some car tires, but they got caught. In jail, the police allowed Ron one phone call—he chose my Mom and Dad for help. Mom and Dad got Ron out of jail, but I did not see him. Mom and Dad loved Ron very much even though he was not adopted. They always referred to Butchie as their "son."

When I was in my first year of college, Dad bought me an old Rambler station wagon, with standard transmission, to commute to school. The car's engine burned oil—blue smoke puffed out of the exhaust pipe whenever I shifted gears. Ron worked at a gas service station then and I visited his station for fill-ups. So, he offered to overhaul the engine—replace the piston rings and valve seats. When he finished working on my car, he picked me up at my house, and drove us to the station. While there, one of his friends stopped at the station. Butchie introduced me as his "Little Eared-Brother" to his friend.

Ron told me that he had been a Boy Scout and that he had gotten into archery. One of his merit projects was to carve a wooden bow from a long, slender tree limb. One winter day, he visited me and gave me his wooden bow. I hung it up on my bedroom wall—I never used it.

A few months later that spring, he visited me again. This time he gave me his used, laminated, full recurve hunting bow—it was beautiful. He said that he had bought a new one for a hunting trip he was planning. He suggested that I practice shooting during the summer, and maybe we would go deer hunting together in the fall. I did practice, and bought a subscription to *ARCHERY* magazine.

That fall, Butchie invited me to go with him and a friend on a bow-and-arrow hunting trip for white-tail deer. We did not get any deer, but I enjoyed being with my big brother again. We played pool and drank a few beers. He told me stories of his hunting trip to Indiana to archery hunt for wild boar. He had been chased up a tree by the boar. While in the tree, Butchie managed to shoot the boar dead.

Ron later became a sheet-metal worker and did jobs for many local shops. He ended his career at the Chrysler Corporation. He enjoyed walking his dogs, cooking, hunting, and fishing. Ron married, raised two boys, divorced, remarried and divorced again. After his first divorce, Ron lived with a guy friend for a while. However, Ron had a white dog that the friend did not care for. So, Ron moved in with our sister Kathy and her husband on their horse farm for several months. He then lived with Father until he met his second wife.

I continued to see Butchie off and on through the years.

SISTER KATHY

Kathy was nine years old and in the house with Mother on THAT DAY for me. Kathy saw the Social Services lady take me away. A few days later, she experienced her own THAT DAY. The Social Services lady took Kathy to a foster family with three boys. Her foster parents had always wanted a little girl to raise. However, Kathy described herself as a tomboy.

Before our family separation, she enjoyed hanging around with Ron and his friends, and playing baseball. Kathy stayed with that foster family for only about six months, when she asked to leave. It was a terrible experience. The oldest boy kept bothering her and trying to kiss her. She finally kicked him in the crotch—he then stopped bothering her.

Social Services then took Kathy to a new foster family, where our baby sister Janet was also living. Those foster parents had one biological daughter of their own. Kathy was cared for, but never adopted. Kathy stayed there until her junior year of high school. At that time, she was around 16 and met our older sister Judy, who was 20, and moved into Judy's apartment until she graduated from high school.

After high school, Kathy married and raised three children. She and her husband maintained a horse farm for over 30 years. The farm was about 10 acres, had an indoor riding facility, and stables for boarding other people's horses. They had one stallion for breeding, and lots of other animals: one pig, one buffalo, one turkey, and chickens. They would occasionally put on horse shows at community events.

When our brother Ron divorced the first time, he lived with Kathy and her husband for several months. Ron had a white dog that enjoyed the farm.

Unfortunately, Kathy's husband died of a heart attack after 35 years of happy marriage. Kathy then sold the farm. I had no contact with Kathy until many years later.

In later years, Kathy told me some things about our biological family life together. We were a very poor family. Father liked to garden, and raised lots of vegetables every summer. He also enjoyed baking bread. Kathy never saw Father drinking beer at home.

Mother suffered from seizures about once a month, her entire life. Each episode would last a few minutes. Father showed Kathy how to place a clothes pin (scissors-style with spring) on Mother's tongue to prevent choking, or biting her tongue. When Mother sensed a seizure attack, Kathy would put a clothes pin on Mother's tongue, and then collect Janet and me on the living room couch to protect us from Mother's flailing arms. Placing the clothes pin on Mother's tongue was like trying to hit a moving target—one time Kathy clipped Mother's lip instead.

After Mother and Father separated, Kathy was the caretaker for us—we were the youngest. Usually, the only ones home were Kathy, Janet, and me. Mother was never home. When Janet or I said that we were hungry, Kathy would go in the kitchen, open the cabinet doors, but only find mice running around—no food.

Kathy hauled Janet and me around in our four-wheeled wagon to collect glass soda bottles (no plastic then), and take them to the neighborhood grocery store for deposit money. She used the money to buy a loaf of bread and lard. She made lard sandwiches for us.

One time, Kathy bought some cookie dough and made chocolate chip cookies. She stored the cookies on the top shelf of the kitchen cabinet. Unfortunately, the next day, she saw that mice had eaten most of them.

(My sister Marlene told me that she never saw any mice in the house, and doubts that Kathy placed a clothes pin on Mother's tongue. Kathy responded that Marlene was never home—she was always at her boyfriend's house, down the street.)

After Mother and Father divorced, Mother re-married. One day she fell and hit her head on a table and died from a seizure attack.

Our house had five bedrooms: One for Jackie, one for Marlene, one for Judy, one shared by Allen and Ron, and one for the baby crib. In the winter, there were not enough blankets in the house for everyone, so Kathy would snuggle up with Janet and me in the crib to keep warm— no covers. (My sister Marlene questions why Kathy had no covers.) The house had two floors with an external stairway to the second floor. With winter snow, the older kids would slide down the steps on pieces of corrugated cardboard.

Kathy remembered that at Christmas time, Uncle Frederick would pick up all of us kids, take us to church, and then to Grandma's for dinner and presents. Dinner consisted of egg salad and ham salad sandwiches, *sulze* (a gelatinous, German, beef and pork, sausage-style dish made in a loaf pan), sugar cookies, and gingerbread cookies.

Kathy also remembered that our two oldest sisters, Jackie and Marlene, argued a lot—they disliked each other all of their lives. Marlene did not attend Jackie's funeral. Jackie had a lot of friends, but sometimes she apparently had a very mean temper.

Why did our parents divorce? Kathy told me that Mother was a "party girl." Father was a lot older than Mother. Mother liked to drink alcohol, and frequented a nearby tavern after their separation. Mother never worked. One time, Kathy and us kids returned home from the store to find Mother naked on the living room couch with a strange man—not Father.

After the divorce, we were on welfare. One time, Kathy saw Mother sitting in front of a mirror, combing her hair. Kathy told Mother that the kids (Janet and I) were hungry, and Kathy needed some money to buy food. No response from Mother. So Kathy found Mother's purse, grabbed a roll of money, and ran upstairs to hide the money in a hole in the wall. When Mother noticed the missing money, she got really mad and yelled at Kathy.

Shortly after the divorce, Mother re-married, and all the kids except Jackie were taken away or left to fend for themselves.

BROTHER ALLEN

Allen was six years old on THAT DAY for me. Allen lived with Father for a while. Then he lived with Ron and me in Crestview for a while. After leaving my foster parents and me in Crestview, Allen went to another foster family, and was adopted. He changed his first name to Tom, but I still called him Allen. We had no contact until he visited me one day after finishing his basic training in the Army. He was 18; I was maybe 15 years old. It was great to see him. He showed me some self-defense moves from his military training. I then used his techniques when wrestling with neighbor kids. I did not see him again for many years.

Allen met his wife while serving in the Army during what the U.S. Government referred to as the "Vietnam Conflict" (not an officially declared war). It was our government's failed attempt to halt the expansion of Communism from North Vietnam to Southeast Asia. The U.S. involvement in the civil war started with military advisors only to South Vietnam in 1959. In 1965, the U.S. expanded its commitment by instituting a military draft and sending thousands of troops as a "police action" to support a corrupt South Vietnam government.

Because of the dense jungle environment in Vietnam, the U.S. military applied a toxic defoliant agent called "Agent Orange" to clear battlefields of vegetation for clearer vision. Unfortunately, many U.S. soldiers suffered negative health effects from the exposure. Allen died at age 70 from complications of his exposure to Agent Orange, as well as COPD from smoking.

I would later learn that he had married, raised one daughter, and divorced.

SISTER JANET

Janet, one year younger than me on THAT DAY, was sent to a separate foster family, with sister Kathy, for about six months. However, the foster parents were older people and were not able to care for a two-year old child. So, Social Services sent Janet to another foster family on a farm. Janet stayed there for several years until she was old enough to help kill some chickens—she had to hold down the chicken's head while the man chopped off the head.

Janet cried and did not want to experience that anymore, so she ran away. Then she was placed with another foster family that had a goose. They bonded closely—the goose followed Janet everywhere. Again, Janet stayed only a few years. Finally, at age eight, Janet was placed with a loving family who adopted her.

We did not see each other for several years. Then, one day, I was maybe nine years old, my Mom said that my sister Janet was coming to visit me. What a surprise! The neighboring Crestview house on one side of our property was another one of the unique, original summer cottages—it was named the "Butterfly House" because it had a double-pitched roof with several large front floor-to-ceiling vertical windows.

By chance, the neighbors who were renting the house were related to Janet's adoptive family. After Mom got to know the neighbors, she contacted Janet's family for a visit. The only thing I remember of the visit is that we talked, and Janet signed her name on one leg of my green octopus doll. I would not see Janet again for many years.

Many years later, Janet shared some of her family experiences with me. She did not remember meeting Mother at Grandma's house during a Christmas gathering. However, sister Jackie told her that Mother did meet Janet and me then—it was after Mother and Father divorced. Janet did remember visiting me in Crestview and signing my green octopus doll.

Janet has no memory of our Mother or sister Judy—they never met. While in high school, one day, she started walking home from after school. A burgundy-colored car stopped beside her. The driver rolled down the car window and asked if she wanted a ride. The driver was our older brother, Ron. He told Janet who he was. She remembered what Ron looked like from our last family gathering at Grandma's when she was about three years old. In addition, Janet had been reminded by sister Kathy and her adopted parents that she had an older brother Ron, but she had had no previous contact with Ron. Janet was surprised and happy to see him.

"Sure," she said. There was another man in the front seat, passenger side. So, Janet climbed in the back seat.

Ron then asked Janet, "Do you know who this man is?"

Janet and the man looked at each other. Janet did not recognize him. She said, "No."

Ron replied, "He is your father."

Janet then noticed some tears in the man's eyes, but Father said nothing. Janet did not know what to say or what to do. When they got near her house, Janet didn't say anything and got out of the car.

Janet and I attended the same high school (one year apart), but we never bumped into each other—we never knew the other sibling was there!

In later years, Janet developed close relationships with both Kathy and Marlene. Janet has asked Marlene questions about our family. However, Marlene has hesitated, and suggested that Janet just forget our family past—too many sad memories: "Just let it go!"

I would learn, many years later, that Janet had married, raised two children, and divorced. She now lives with her oldest son, and remains friends with her ex-husband.

UNCLE FREDERICK

Uncle Frederick served in the Air Force as a pilot during World War Two, then in the Air Force Reserve until he was 60 years old. After the war, he lived with Grandma until she died. Then, at age of 46, he married his long-time girlfriend. He was employed as a product development engineer in fluid and air filtration at two Racine companies—Walker Manufacturing and Cummins Engine Company.

Uncle Frederick visited me twice. Once, when I was in grade school, he picked me up at my new house in Crestview, and took me to a golf tournament at the Racine Country Club. He drove a convertible, roof-down, car—nice ride! On the golf course, I was so short that I could not see anything through all the people.

Then, when I was 15, he attended my confirmation in the Lutheran church. Most kids are confirmed around the age of 13, but my parents were not very religious. My adopted dad never attended church. Mom and I attended a church in Racine, usually only twice a year—Christmas and Easter.

At about that same age, a new church was built only a few miles away. Mom and I then attended that church regularly, and Mom sang in the choir for a while. I have a nice photograph of Uncle Frederick and me in our front yard that day. When my mom died, he attended the funeral. We talked awhile, exchanged mailing addresses, but had no further contact for many years.

Uncle Frederick & Rick (15 years old)

BIOLOGICAL PARENTS

I have only limited memories of my mother, and no memories of Father. After I was taken away to my foster parents, there was to be no legal contact. I may have met Mother one time, after the separation, at Grandma's house for Christmas—not sure. I later learned that Mother divorced from Father. She re-married, had a daughter named Joy, then died at age 38 (I would have been five). I read an obituary in the newspaper that Father had died at age 77. I was 25. I have no memory of him.

Chapter 7

My Youth Years

Before I started school, I spent lots of time outside playing in a sandbox, and playing with my dog, Jiggers. Mom enjoyed music, and frequently played popular music records all day long: Dean Martin, Perry Como, Frank Sinatra (Mom's favorite), Nat King Cole (my favorite), Patti Page, Doris Day, Peggy Lee, and Kay Star (Dad's favorite). Mom had a large record album collection.

Mom tried to get me to play some musical instrument, but I had no interest. I liked listening to music, but I had no music or artistic talents. In my bedroom, I listened to my Davy Crocket record on my plastic record player: "King of the Wild Frontier." I also enjoyed long hours lying under my bed with a long piece of string that I wove through the bed springs – I was fixing the bed(?).

One day, I was home alone. Mom was shopping, Dad was at work, and I was under my bed. A neighbor lady knocked on the front door, but I did not hear that. The main door was open, so the lady opened the screen door, and called out, "Anyone home?"

I replied, "I'm in here".

"Where are you?", she asked.

"In my bedroom", I said.

She walked into my room, but did not see me. "Where are you?" she asked again.

"Under the bed," I said. She bent down and looked under the bed at me.

"What in the world … Why are you under there?" she exclaimed.

"I am fixing my bed," I said.

"Is your bed broken? Get out of there!" she ordered.

So, I crawled out from under my bed, and told her, "My bed is NOT broken. I just like to play under there."

While growing up in Crestview, I became a nature kid. Almost every day, the neighborhood kids and I played in the nearby woods, climbed trees, played in the stream at the bottom of the ravine, watched birds, and picked wild berries and flowers. When not in the woods, we were down on the beach. Sometimes we climbed down the bluffs to the beach, which was always challenging because of erosion and mud pockets after heavy rains. However, we normally walked down to the beach along the access road on the side of the ravine.

The annual die-offs of alewives were really terrible some years. The dead fish piled up on the beach by the tons – really smelly odor!

In the summer, several neighborhood kids and I would frequently campout overnight. Mosquitos and flies were ubiquitous. We did not have insect repellent – we just tried to swat them away. Most days, I ended up with red welts all over me. Sometimes, we held "biting" contests. We each would hold out our arms to let mosquitos land and bite us. We would watch as the bugs swelled up with blood, and almost turned red in color. Who could get the largest bug swell? Then, just as the bug started to fly off – SPLAT, one of us would smack it, splattering blood in the air. Great laughs! Playing at the sand pits was also great fun: riding our bikes up and down the hills, and catching frogs in the ponds.

I learned to be an environmentalist, even before I knew it. When I was a young kid, recycling glass containers was routine. Empty soda bottles were returned to the grocery store for deposit, and empty milk jugs were picked up by the milk man each week when he delivered fresh milk from the truck. Dad taught me to compost food scraps, and yard waste for the garden. While enjoying my ventures in the woods, hunting or just walking, the sight of occasional trash made me sad – why do people litter?

One time at college, I was driving to school with a classmate. He was drinking a can of soda in my car. When the can was empty, he rolled down the car window and started to throw the can out of the window. I yelled at him, "STOP!"

He was startled. "What's wrong?" he asked.

I asked him to just drop the can on the car floor, and NOT throw it out of the window. He was surprised at my sensitivity to his careless action. Over the years, I have spent many hours picking up roadside and streamside litter, by myself and with Adopt-A-Highway and Adopt-A-Stream groups. I wish that more people would cherish the beauty in nature, and try to preserve our natural habitat, rather than trash it or destroy it.

In the spring time, smelt fishing on the Lake Michigan shoreline was a popular nighttime activity. Smelt are small fish, less than 10 inches in length, and very tasty. Large schools swim in near the shoreline at night. Two capture techniques were used. Some people used a sein net, with two people on opposites ends, walking through the shallow water to try and scoop up the small fish. Other people used a large, square, dip-net hung by a rope at the end of a long wooden pole. The dip-net set-up was supported on a tripod stand, fixed in one place, and required only one person to operate. We would typically go home with a five-gallon bucket full of fish. Dad always offered to share some of our catch with neighbors.

In the fall, I learned to go hunting and trap shooting with Dad. We hunted in the nearby Crestview woods and fields for cotton-tailed rabbits and ring-necked pheasants. There was always an acrid odor in the air during October from rotten cabbage plants left in the nearby farm fields after the heads had been harvested.

We also travelled to north-central Wisconsin to hunt for ruffed grouse and white-tailed deer. Dad had a small gun collection, consisting of an old 30-30 Winchester, lever-action rifle (inherited from Grandpa Burt, but still accurate); a 12-gauge pump shotgun; a 16-gauge double barrelled shotgun; a 410-gauge bolt-action shotgun; a single-shot, 22-gauge bolt-action rifle; and an old Italian military, 6.5 mm bolt-action rifle.

We used two methods for cleaning game birds. One method required plucking the feathers from the skin – that took some effort, and was time-consuming, but left the skin and fat on the bird for cooking. The other method was to skin the bird. We would hang the bird upside down by its feet, make knife cuts around the legs, and pull down on the skin, feathers intact—no skin or fat left on the meat.

In the winter, we took our sleds for rides down the snowy ravine slopes. Ice skating on the frozen ponds at the sand pits was fun. Sometimes we even tried to play hockey games. When the weather got really cold (below zero Fahrenheit), we explored the huge ice caves on the beach, and ventured out on the partially frozen lake. That was really stupid, because the ice coverage was really rough, and Lake Michigan is very cold and very deep.

Some winters were colder than others, and had more snowfall. When I was in grade school, I dug many caves through the snow packs in the front yard. One time, the overnight snow fall was so heavy that Dad could not drive the car out of the driveway in the morning; the snow banks were way over my head. We spent many hours shoveling snow out of the driveway. Some neighbors eventually got snow-blowers, but not us.

One winter, the February temperature stayed very cold for two weeks straight – less than 20 degrees below zero Fahrenheit, lots of ground snow and very windy! I could hear our house make creaking noises from the wind. Dad would not let Mom out of the house – not even to walk to the mailbox by the front road. Mom got "cabin fever" and started hallucinating—they argued a lot. I thought they were going to get divorced. Fortunately, the weather eventually warmed up and Mom recovered.

Starting when I was probably ten years old, I routinely got scaled-plastic model assembly kits as gifts for birthdays and Christmas. I enjoyed the challenge of following the instructions, and gluing the many pieces together to create a whole something.

One was a nine-cylinder, propeller airplane engine, with a small electric motor that moved the pistons, valves, and propeller. The cylinders were made of clear plastic to allow view of the piston and valve movements. Tiny red light bulbs simulated spark plugs.

Another "action" model was a "Chrysler Slant-6" car engine – again with clear plastic to view the action of pistons, valves, and spark plugs (red lights). I also assembled several ships: an aircraft carrier, a battleship, and two sail ships, plus some model cars and airplanes. Dad installed a long shelf along one wall of my bedroom to display all of the models. I proudly showed friends, and other visitors, my model collection. Unfortunately, Mom did not like how they all collected dust.

I wonder whatever happened to all those models?

Dad taught me how to throw and catch a baseball. I developed a very good throwing arm, and became the team pitcher in Little League, Pony League, and on my high school team. Dad taught me how to throw a curve ball and a knuckle ball. We played catch in the backyard often, until one day when I was in high school. I was practicing pitching to Dad catching, in a crouched position. I threw a curve ball. Dad moved his glove, but failed to catch the sharply breaking pitch. The ball missed his glove, glanced off his knee, and landed in his crotch – ouch! Dad fell forward and did a face-plant on the ground. When I reached him, he rolled over, and told me that he was through catching for me.

Santa Claus?

When I was about six or seven years old, Santa Claus walked into our house. It was Christmas Eve. I was worried that Santa might not visit me that year because there was no snow on the ground. I was in bed and had just fallen asleep when Mom woke me up. She said that Santa Claus was here to give me presents. I was confused – I thought that Santa came down the chimney, left presents, ate the cookies that we had left out for him, and then left. Why did he want to meet me?

Mom grabbed my bathrobe, pulled me out of bed, and helped me into the robe. We then walked into the living room, where Dad was standing by the front door. Dad opened the door and there stood Santa in a red suit with a large black belt around his middle, tall black boots, long white beard, and red Santa hat.

But why was Santa wearing a plastic face mask? Was he really Santa Claus?

Santa walked into our house, dropped his sack and pulled out my presents. He wished me a Merry Christmas and left. Before opening my presents, I asked Mom and Dad, "How could Santa get here with no snow on the ground? How could his reindeer fly with no snow? Why did I not see his sleigh and reindeer? Why was Santa wearing a plastic face mask? Was he really Santa Claus?"

Mom and Dad said that Santa had other ways to get around that year.

"Open your presents," they said.

Of course, I later realized that a neighbor was playing Santa Claus. There was no more talk of Santa Claus at future Christmases.

FIRST HALLOWEEN

My first Halloween was a real trip – actually! Mom asked some older neighborhood kids to take me along. I wore a costume with a plastic facemask and could barely see through the eye holes. I carried a plastic jack-o-lantern to collect my goodies.

We started walking the roads of the neighborhood. However, another group of kids told us about one house that was giving out really nice goodies, but the supply was limited. So, my chaperones took off running across the open fields and through some house construction sites. They yelled at me to keep up, but I was too slow. They jumped over an open trench, but I did not see it. Down I went, face first. I yelled for help with some tears in my eyes. They came back to pull me up, then took me home. They then continued "trick-or-treating" without me.

PET DOGS

Over the years, I had several pets. Before fostering me, Mom and Dad got a Brittany Spaniel dog from Grandpa Burt. He named it "Jiggers" (because the puppy wiggled around a lot). Jiggers had large liver-colored and white patches. He was a great hunting dog. When he picked up the scent of wild game, he began barking non-stop until the animal eluded capture, or Dad was able to shoot the animal.

When not hunting, I took Jiggers for daily walks in the nearby woods or down to the beach. One time, some friends and I were eating a bag of potato chips. Jiggers was watching us closely. So, we gave him one chip. He inhaled it. We gave him another, and another, until his mouth began to foam over. We laughed, and decide that we had better stop feeding him.

When Jiggers got older, Mom and Dad decided that I needed a puppy – another Brittany Spaniel dog. I named it "Bunky" – I think from a cartoon character. I was in grade school and enjoyed that little critter for about a week, but he had a short life.

Mom took care of the puppy while I was at school. One day, I came home after school, and Mom was sitting on the couch, crying. Mom told me that she had been house cleaning and had opened the front door for a while. Bunky decided to run out the open door. Mom tried to run after him, but he was too fast. Bunky mistakenly ran behind a neighbor's car that was backing out of the driveway. Bunky did not survive. The neighbor apologized. Mom was devastated.

Of course, I was sad. Mom bought me some goldfish one time, but I was not really interested. I failed to feed them and clean the glass bowl often enough – they did not survive. Mom then tried some parakeets. They lasted only a few weeks before they managed to fly out an open door (or window?).

I was in high school when Jiggers died. By coincidence, a neighbor had to move away, and gave us his hunting dog, "Missy Sue." She was a Springer Spaniel, with black and white patches. Missy was a terrific hunting dog.

One day, a neighborhood friend and I took Missy down to the beach for a walk. We would pick up pieces of driftwood and throw them as far out in the lake as we could. Missy loved to swim out to retrieve the floating wood. We also liked to pick up flat rocks, and throw them across the water to see how many times we could skip the rock. Missy usually did not chase after the skipping rocks. However, one time she apparently got confused, and swam out after a skipping rock. We yelled after her to come back – no response. We then threw pieces of wood out to distract her, but those were no help. She kept swimming out.

My friend had a hunting dog, a Labrador retriever, named "Night." He decided to run home to get Night. I stayed on the beach, yelling for Missy to come back. When my friend returned, Missy was so far out in the lake we could hardly see her black head. Night jumped in the water, and swam out to Missy. It was an amazing sight. That dog caught up to Missy, and the two dogs swam back to shore. We both hugged our two very wet, tired dogs. We were much more careful with Missy at the beach after that.

VACATIONS

When I was maybe five years old, Mom and I took a train ride to visit Aunt Myrtle in Tulsa, Oklahoma. It was an overnight trip, so we had a sleeper car. Mom and I were in a top berth. However, I was so excited to keep looking out the window that I did not want to sleep. Mom got mad at me for keeping her awake all night.

After visiting Tulsa for a few days, Mom and I rented a car and drove over the Ozark Plateau and Boston Mountains to Little Rock, Arkansas, to visit Aunt Hazel and Uncle Red. Again, I was so excited to look at the

beautiful scenery that I was no help to Mom for naviga-
tion. We got lost, or turned around, several times; Mom
was NOT happy. In Little Rock, I tasted natural hot spring
water – interesting!

On our return trip to Wisconsin, we boarded a two-
engine, propeller airplane. Mom called it a "puddle
jumper." I did not like the ride, especially during takeoff,
and when the plane hit an "air pocket." Mom tried to
explain that there was no problem, but my stomach
disagreed. We landed safely in Milwaukee.

At first, Dad got one week vacation each summer,
then after several years, he got two weeks' vacation. Each
year, Mom would invite a different neighborhood kid to
join us, for my benefit. We always first drove north for
about five hours to Antigo to visit Grandpa Burt. Then, we
proceeded another hour to a small rural town called
Kempster. There, we turned off the paved road and
followed a dirt road for about a mile through forest and
swamp land to Lower Bass Lake. It is a beautiful little
fresh water lake, with an hour-glass shape, of three
sections—great for fishing and swimming. The resort
owner, Joe, operated a tavern at one end of the lake, and
rented out three rustic cabins for fishermen and hunters.
No plumbing. We had to carry buckets of water from a
nearby hand-pump well. Each cabin had an outhouse.

Mom and Dad loved to fish all day, from early
morning to dark. As bait we usually used minnows,
worms or artificial lures. We mostly caught smaller
pan-fish: bluegills, crappie and yellow perch, with an

occasional small-sized large-mouth bass. Large-mouth bass are strong fighting fish, that will jump out of the water when hooked.

One time, while talking with Joe about fishing, he suggested that if we wanted to catch a really big large-mouth bass, we should try frogs as bait.

"Where do we get frogs?" I asked.

He replied, "Jump in my truck." He drove me to a nearby lake with a marsh area. Old Joe showed me how to get down on my hands and knees and grab the frogs. We caught several little green frogs. Joe said that the smaller frogs were best for fishing. He explained that for bait, you need to squeeze the air out of the frog, and then pass a hook through its lips.

The next day, Mom tried using one of the bait frogs. By surprise, she caught hold of a BIG large-mouth bass. Over the years, she loved to repeat the story of how she struggled for a long time fighting that jumping five–pound fish – she was so proud of that catch.

We used two methods for cleaning caught fish. The first method might be called "scale and gut". First, we used a toothed scaling tool to remove the scales from the fish's skin. Then, we used a knife to slit the fish's belly, remove the internal organs, and cut off the head. This method left the skin and bones on the fish for cooking.

The other method is called "filleting." You need a thin-bladed, very sharp knife. First, you cut vertically downward behind the head and gills. Then, you carefully cut along the backbone and ribcage to remove the meat. Next, you start at the tail end, and carefully slice away the skin from the flesh. No need to scale or remove the guts.

One late evening, it was almost dark when we ended fishing. We had a stringer full of pan-fish. Dad suggested tying the stringer to the dock, leave the fish in the water overnight, and then clean the fish in the morning.

The next morning, I walked onto the wooden dock and felt a large splash under my feet, and then a large swirl of water out from under the dock. It was a big snapping turtle! I then pulled up the stringer, but only fish heads were left. The turtle had had a nice meal. After that, Dad brought a fish basket to keep caught fish in.

When I was in high school, Mom and Dad purchased a wooded lot near a man-made lake formed by a hydroelectric dam on the Wisconsin River called Castle Rock Lake. They chose that site since Dad and I went hunting in that area every fall. They bought a used house trailer and moved it onto the lot. One summer vacation, we invited a school friend, Mike, to join us.

Mike was a mischievous kid. One evening, Mike and I walked down to the lake to go fishing. We spotted a large, dead fish on the shoreline (about a 10-pound muskie). Mike convinced me to help carry that fish (we shoved a long stick through its gills) to the local pavilion, which served as a dance hall/restaurant/ tavern building. We placed the fish at the front entrance. Mike just happened to have a smoke bomb with him. He lit off the smoke bomb, and we ran to a nearby safe hiding place to watch people walk out the door, through the smoke and stepping over that fish – we could not stop laughing! The next day, Mom and Dad heard about the incident, and questioned us – we pleaded innocent.

Castle Rock Lake is very large. In stormy weather, the waves can get nasty. One time, Mom, Dad, and I were fishing for walleye in our boat on the lake when a storm suddenly rose up. Dad fired up the motor and we headed for shore. However, the waves got very rough and we were surrounded by white caps. Mom became disoriented, and tried to jump out of the boat. Dad and I just barely managed to catch Mom before she hit the water. Boy, that was close!

Another time, Dad and I were drift-fishing for walleye, with four lines in the water. (Wisconsin fishing regulations allow each person to have two lines in the water). One of Dad's lines plunged down quickly and crossed over all the other lines. It was a big fish. We naturally thought that it must be a muskie. Muskies can be very large game fish.

It took us a long while to reel in that fish, but what was it? It was one ugly fish! Neither Dad nor I could identify it. When we got to shore, we drove to a bait and tackle store. We showed the fish to several people. One guy identified it as a dogfish. We had never heard of that species and were told not to eat it, but to bury it.

When I was in high school, Dad and I were invited by neighborhood friends to go to Crandon to hunt for white-tailed deer, a popular fall tradition in Wisconsin. They had a rustic cabin on about 40 acres of wooded land. Crandon is in the rural, northern part of the state. Dad and I had not been there before. The weather was very cold: 20 degrees below zero Fahrenheit! There was only a small amount of snow on the ground – deer hunters like ground snow for easier tracking and quieter walking.

Late one afternoon, Dad and I were walking through the woods within sight of each other. Then, Dad motioned for me to stop, raised his rifle and shot once. Dad was usually an accurate, one-shot hunter. The deer collapsed, then jumped up and bounded off. We walked to the spot where the deer had initially fallen.

We found no blood. Dad said he must have hit the buck in its antlers, and only shocked it. We separated again, in hopes of surrounding the deer. After walking for a while, I stopped. I could no longer see Dad. I called out—no response. Again, no answer. I looked around—nothing but trees. I was lost. Dad had taught me to always take a compass reading before entering a large forest, but we had not done that today. The sky was overcast, so I couldn't get my bearings from the sun.

Which way was North? Which way should I walk? I managed to cross an old logging road. So, I followed it out of the woods to the edge of a farm field. I crossed the field to a paved road. I looked in both directions. I had no idea where I was. I unloaded my rifle, and started walking down the road. It would turn out to be the wrong direction! Maybe a car or truck would pass by.

After walking a while, it started to get dark. No cars or trucks. I thought about Dad; I hoped that he made it back to the cabin okay. Then, by luck, I spotted a pickup truck backing out of the woods on a logging road. I asked the driver for a ride. Did he know where our friends' cabin was? He did! It was on the other side of the woods. I had walked the wrong way.

I climbed into the truck, relieved to have found a way out of my mishap. It was totally dark now. After about a 15-minute ride, the driver stopped the truck at the driveway to the cabin. I thanked the driver and ran down the long driveway. Dad was outside, shooting his rifle into the air to attract my attention. Then he spotted me and ran toward me. We hugged each other. We shared lots of hunting stories that night. Dad blamed himself for my getting lost, but I knew it was my fault.

FOSTER BROTHER

When I was in grade school (I do not remember my age), Mom and Dad fostered another boy about my age, whose name was Buddy. We looked like twins – both of us had butch haircuts with blonde hair, and were the same height and weight. Buddy stayed with us for about one school season. I never knew why he was with us, but I enjoyed his companionship. Then, he left. I never saw him again.

School Days

I did not attend kindergarten. Mom set me on her lap and read to me a few times. Mom and Dad bought me a set of children's encyclopedia books with lots of colorful pictures. They taught me the alphabet, how to print my name, and how to count to 20. I was ready for school, or, so I thought. However, I had little contact with other kids before attending school.

At the Crestview school, first and second grades were together in one classroom. I was an antsy student and could not sit still. I wanted to be outside running around. Practicing printing letters on lined paper was NOT my forte. "Keep the letters between the lines," the teacher barked at us.

I got only average grades, and several critical comments on my report card: Poor writing skills and inattentiveness. In later years, Mom told me that the teacher suggested that I repeat first grade. Apparently, I was a "slow learner," and not ready for second grade. Mom pleaded with the teacher to not hold me back. So, I advanced with my class to second grade.

In second grade, the teacher one day asked each student to stand up in front of the class, and talk about their family heritage. At home, when looking in the bathroom mirror, I had noticed that I had deep-set, squinty eyes—different from most other people. I had seen pictures in magazines and my encyclopedia of some foreign people with squinty eyes. So, in class that day I said that I was Chinese. Of course, everyone laughed, because all of the other kids, and the teacher, were of European descent. That evening, the teacher called my Mom about my comment in class. Mom got deeply upset with me. She told me, "You are not Chinese! Stop telling people that!" I managed to pass second grade.

In third grade, I did not finish an arithmetic test for long-addition, but I got the correct answer for the problems that I completed. My best friend, Ralph, finished the test, and got a perfect 100 score. Again, I was labelled by the teacher as a "slow learner."

Mom and Dad were deeply disappointed in me. "You must do better," they told me. I eventually managed to get a "B" grade in arithmetic – my first above-average grade in any subject! All other subject grades were just average. My reading and writing skills were poor.

Recess was fun. The school campus had a large grass playfield next to the woods and ravine. We often played co-ed kickball and softball. At one end, we dug several small pocket holes in the ground to play "marbles" games. Most kids had a bag of small and large (a.k.a., boulders) glass marbles (and some small steel balls). Some kids' bags were larger than others. There was a large swing-set, jungle gym, monkey-bars and a merry-go-round table. One area was asphalt covered with two basketball goals, but no court lines.

In fourth grade, I still did not know how to swim. So, my best friend, Ralph, and I were enrolled in the local YMCA. Our parents agreed to alternate driving us the ten miles into Racine to the Y on Saturday mornings. We were there from 9:00 am, through lunch, until about 3:00 p.m. It was great fun! We would first have a gym session for an hour, then pool time for an hour. There were two indoor swimming pools—a deep pool and a shallow pool. We were initially assigned to the "Minnow D" class, for beginner and non-swimmers, in the shallow pool.

After a month or so, the swim instructor told us that we were going to have a swimming test to measure our progress. If we passed, we would move up to "Minnow C" class, or higher. Both Ralph and I did well. We were advanced to the "Minnow A" class. Yeah! The instructor then offered us a bigger challenge. If we wanted, we could test in the deep pool to advance to the "Shark" class. I agreed. Ralph said "NO". He was satisfied to stay in the shallow pool. I tried to encourage him to try the test with me but he refused. I got frustrated with him, and called him a chicken. I then walked to the deep pool with the instructor, swam the test, and passed. I was a Shark.

When Ralph's mother picked us up that day, she asked why we were so quiet. No response from either of us. When I got home, I did not talk with Mom about the swim test. Then, the phone rang. It was Ralph's mom. She told Mom that I had called Ralph a chicken and that he was emotionally hurt. Mom hung up the phone, and asked me to explain. She was not happy. Mom congratulated me on my successful swim test, but asked me what we were going to do now that Ralph and I were in different swim classes. She suggested that I apologize to Ralph to save our friendship. I said, "No, he is a chicken. It is his fault for not testing with me". That was the end of our friendship. Ralph and I never reconciled, and were unfriendly to each other the rest of our school days.

Just before Christmas vacation, the school teacher played a musical record for a ballet called, "The Nutcracker." I had never heard such incredible music. My favorite part was called "The Waltz of the Flowers." Whenever I hear that music, memories of childhood flood through me! At the end of the school year (springtime), our class visited the Racine Heritage Museum for our field trip. I learned a lot about my hometown during that trip.

In fifth grade, I studied the map of the USA, the states and state capital cities. I liked that! Again I got a "B" grade in arithmetic. However, my reading and writing skills were still poor. That year, I remember many snowball fights on winter mornings before school. We formed two long lines "military style" about ten feet apart on an empty field across the street from the school. Snowball throwing was not allowed on school property. We pelted each other until the bell rang to start school. I had a good throwing arm.

The class field trip that year was to the Chicago Museum of Science & Industry. What a great trip! On the bus ride there, we all sang the song, "One hundred bottles of beer on the wall." Two major memories: Going down into the coal mine, and seeing the inside of a submarine.

In sixth grade, during fall and spring warm weather for recess, we played a lot of co-ed kickball and softball. However, during the winter, the boys always played touch football, even in the cold and snow.

In the spring, at the end of the school year, we all took an achievement test. I scored just average in all subjects. The smartest kid in class, Jimmy, scored very well in all subjects. He qualified for accelerated classes when we transitioned to seventh grade and junior high school. I was very jealous! Jimmy and I lived on the same road—Paul Bunyan Road. So, we would often walk to and from school together.

He once told me that he planned to go to college to be a psychiatrist.

"What is that?" I asked. He said that it was a special medical doctor who treated people with mental problems. I had no idea what I wanted to do with my life. I really had no ambition. However, my parents both encouraged me to study in school, and try to get good grades. They wanted me to attend college – whatever that was. Neither Mom nor Dad had had the opportunity to attend college.

So, for seventh grade, instead of attending my community school, I walked about a half mile to catch the school bus to the junior high school in Racine, about five miles away. Whew, was that a crowded school! Classrooms were completely full, and hallways were literally shoulder-to-shoulder walking between classes. I continued to get "B" grades in arithmetic (math) class, but only average grades in other classes, even gym class, through eighth grade.

When I was 13 years old, I got my first job—a paper route. I walked around the community delivering the *Racine Journal Times* newspaper door-to-door. I did that for about one year.

In the spring, summer, and fall, I also worked on two nearby farms. Springtime was for picking strawberries, and planting cabbage and potato plants. Summer was for weeding and hoeing. Fall was for harvesting: Bagging cabbage and potatoes, and tossing the bags up onto a wagon was tough work! The potatoes had been dug-up by a mechanical digger and let laid out on the ground to dry.

Then, in ninth grade, something clicked in me. Apparently, I was academically what some people call a "late bloomer." I have often wondered if my delayed academic achievements were caused by poor nutrition during my first three years, or from exposure to secondhand tobacco smoke in my later childhood.

The website for the Centers for Disease Control (cdc.gov) lists many negative health effects from secondhand smoke. I got my first "A" grade: Algebra 1 math class. Plus, several "B" grades in other classes. I had some excellent teachers who contributed to my improvement. That year in civics class, we took another achievement test. I scored high in math, but only average in other subjects. I still had poor reading and writing skills.

One class project was for each student to do library research on possible vocations of interest. Of course, there was no Internet then. I decided on engineering. At home, I discussed the project with Mom and Dad. Mom asked me what type of engineering.

"What type?" I thought. "Oh, I want to design cars. Isn't that mechanical engineering?" I replied. Mom suggested that I look at chemical engineering. The previous Christmas, Santa Claus had given me an experimental chemistry set. Mom thought that I would enjoy chemistry and physics subjects when I entered high school. So, I planned on studying chemical engineering.

The last four weeks of spring classes, the gym teacher told us that we were to be introduced to the game of tennis. "Tennis," I thought. "Do boys play tennis?"

The school had three concrete tennis courts. The teacher explained some of the rules and strategy of the game. He then led us into a large equipment storage closet. On one wall were hanging a group of tennis rackets —all steel framed, with braided steel strings. The gym teacher told us to try handling several of different sizes to see which felt most comfortable to us. He then opened several pressurized cans of white tennis balls. We tried playing. I found it to be great fun! I got hooked on the sport.

A few days later, I bought my first tennis racket for $4 at a Target discount store—a wooden Dunlap Max Ply.

I spent many hours hitting tennis balls against school brick walls, and occasionally playing tennis with friends.

When I was about 15, a neighbor had a commercial packaging business in Racine. He invited me, with other neighborhood kids, and his son, to work at his shop. I continued to work full-time during the summer, on Saturdays during school, and on holidays through my sophomore year of college. I managed to put most of my earnings into a bank savings account for my college education.

In high school, I really improved as a student. I aced chemistry, physics, and math classes. Much to my surprise, I also aced English classes, probably, again, because of GREAT teachers. My writing skills improved; however, I was still a slow reader. I got only a "C" grade in biology, but I liked the class. I had difficulty reading and understanding the textbook.

During my senior year, one night after dinner, Mom and Dad asked me if I had thought about college. I had thought, some. I had talked with a guidance counselor at school. After arriving at school each morning, I headed to the school library to look through the many college yearbooks, including University of Wisconsin. Wow, college life looked really exciting.

Mom then mentioned that my parents could not afford to send me to a university. She suggested an alternative. Mom and Dad would LET me live at home, no room or board charges, IF I agreed to attend the local two-year college: UW – Racine Extension. Plus, they would pay for my tuition. I had to buy my own text books and school supplies. However, for my junior and senior college years, I would need to transfer to the University campus in Madison to complete my bachelor's degree. I would then have to pay my own tuition, books, housing and living expenses out of my savings.

At first, I was a little stunned. It never occurred to me that once I turned 18, my parents were no longer legally responsible for my welfare. They could have kicked me out of the house and wished me good luck (like what my Dad had experienced). After pondering the possible consequences, I said, "Yeah, deal. Thanks!"

The summer following high school graduation, I worked full-time, and played my last season of league baseball. I also enjoyed occasional tennis with friends.

Chapter 8
RON AND ROSE

ROSE WAS ONE OF THE GIRLS IN the neighborhood who was a close friend with my biological family. (See Chapter 3.) After high school, she was a waitress at a restaurant that my brother Ron frequented. The first time I met Rose, I was 16. I was walking to the school bus stop on a cold, snowy winter morning. A burgundy-colored car pulled past me and stopped.

There were two people in the car—a man and a woman. The driver rolled down the window, and asked me if I wanted a ride—it was my big brother Butchie! I climbed into the car next to the woman. Ron introduced me to Rose. She was very pretty with long, black hair. At school, I was walking on a cloud all day—my big brother had given me a ride to school!

The second time I met Rose was when Ron brought her to my Crestview house to visit me, and to meet Mom and Dad. Ron and Rose were planning to get married. Rose and Mom talked in the kitchen, while Butchie, Dad, and I went outside to the garden.

Mom told Rose NOT to marry Ronnie. "He will only hurt you," Mom said. Rose started crying and ran out of the house to us in the garden. Both Ron and Dad tried to console Rose, but she was deeply hurt. Mom never apologized for her comment to Rose, although they would develop a very close, loving relationship.

About a year later, when I was 17, Ron asked me to be an attendant in his wedding with Rose. Ron was 25; Rose was 18. They invited me to some rehearsal parties before the wedding. I met Rose's three sisters and Rose's parents.

Rose described for me their first date. It had been a double-date with another couple. They decided to buy some beer and go parking in a wooded area. Ron was driving; Rose next to him in the front seat. The other couple was in the back seat, getting really "friendly" with each other. Rose said that Ron was a really great joke-teller, one after another. She could not stop laughing. Everyone was drinking their cans of beer dry and then tossing the empty beer cans out the car window. Rose had never had alcohol before. She took one sip of beer, and did not like the taste. However, she wanted to be "cool." So, she took one more sip from the can, and decided to toss the mostly full beer can out the window.

As luck would have it (Murphy's Law?), Rose had a very accurate throwing arm – the mostly full beer can hit a nearby tree, and went SPLAT! Everyone laughed—except Rose—who was a little embarrassed.

On wedding day, I was standing outside the back of the church with Ron, his best man, Jerry, and the other two attendants waiting for the ceremony to start. I told Ron that I was nervous (a problem I had my whole life).

He asked, "Why are you nervous? I am the one getting married.".

Following the ceremony, we went to a dinner party. Champagne was served. I had never had champagne before and I liked the bubbly taste. However, the next morning, I woke up with a terrific headache. Mom and Dad just laughed at me and said perhaps I should not drink champagne anymore.

The wedding reception was huge – lots of people that I did not know. However, my older sister Jackie was there, quite inebriated, and tried to dance with me. I was not a very good dancer, but I enjoyed her effort. In later years, Rose told me that Ron's father (my biological father) was also at the reception; however, I did not see him and he did not talk with me.

I am glad that I did not encounter my biological father. I may have wanted to punch him in the face for being such an irresponsible father to me. I think that before people initiate the action for giving birth to children, they should make sure that they have adequate LOVE and resources to care for those children—but that is just my opinion.

After their marriage, Rose visited me often. Ron worked nights at the gas service station, and would sometimes drop Rose off at the Crestview house before going to work. She did not like to be alone. Rose and I enjoyed each other's company. She especially enjoyed teasing me about my bowed legs and big ears. Ron picked her up after work.

When I was 20 years old, about two years after my brother Ron and Rose got married, their first child, Robbie, was born. I was still living at home in Wisconsin, attending the local college. Ron often dropped off Rose with the baby at my Crestview house while he went to his night-time work at the gas service station.

Mom and Dad loved the visits as foster grandparents. They called Ron their son, Robbie their grandson; and Rose their daughter-in law. Their marriage confused me. I knew that Ron and Rose loved each other very much. However, they argued a lot, and sometimes made mean faces at each other. They really did not show much affection for each other.

When I was attending school at Madison, Rose gave birth to her second child. Unfortunately, he died at birth. They named him after me, Charles Richard. About a year after that, their third child was born: Timmy.

After I graduated from college and left home, Mom and Dad developed a very close, loving relationship with Rose and the kids. When I came home on Christmas vacations, Mom, Dad, and I would always visit with Ron, Rose, and their kids.

Unfortunately, Ron and Rose separated, and then divorced. Mom told Rose, "I tried to warn you [about Ron]."

RON AND ROSE

Mom, Dad, and I maintained a close relationship with Rose and the kids, but had no further contact with Ron. Rose stayed in the house with the kids. Ron left; I had no idea where he went. Ron never contacted me after the divorce. Rose never told me where Ron was. Rose was so distraught over the divorce and so mad at Ron. She told me several times how much she still loved him. I had lost my big brother Butchie—again! Ron and Rose never reconciled. They have both since re-married.

Chapter 9
MY ADULT YEARS

AFTER HIGH SCHOOL, I ACCEPTED my parents' offer to stay at home and attend the local two-year college, University of Wisconsin—Racine Extension. Before the first day of classes, all freshmen students (about 50) took an entrance exam, went on a short guided tour of the facilities (library, science labs, and one large lecture hall), then gathered in the student lounge for an orientation talk by the administrator. He welcomed us to the college. Then he told us to look at the student on our left, then at the right. "Only one of you will graduate and earn a college degree."

The national statistics for public college freshmen students: 33% graduation rate. That statistic still holds today—by comparison, freshmen students at the University of Wisconsin—Madison campus graduate at 87% rate. I thought to myself, "I did not study my butt off in high school to fail out of college." Fortunately, my college instructors were great teachers. I achieved mostly "A" and "B" grades, with a few "Cs".

During the summer break after my freshmen year, I decided to take a three-credit sociology course, as well as work full time. I noticed that the tuition schedule was one fee for one to two credits, and a slightly higher fee for three to four credits.

"Well," I thought. "Is there a one-credit course that I could essentially take for FREE?" I scanned the syllabus of course offerings. There was one: tennis—my chance to get some professional tennis instruction. There were six concrete tennis courts on the campus. That was a fun class.

There was a similar local college in Kenosha, about ten miles away. That year, the university system decided to merge the two colleges to form the new University of Wisconsin–Parkside campus. During my sophomore year, the first new building was completed in the nearby rural town of Somers. I took a shuttle bus to the new campus for one math class—Calculus III. UW–Parkside (UWP) is now a thriving four-year, degree-granting institution, with over 4,000 students.

UNIVERSITY OF WISCONSIN–MADISON

I declared my major to be Chemical Engineering. This meant the practical application of the principles of math, chemistry, physics, economics, verbal communications, and technical writing to industrial problems. UWP did not offer that major.

Therefore, after my sophomore year, I transferred to the Madison campus to complete my degree. In Madison (also the state capitol), studying engineering courses was interesting, but for me, was not fun—it was a lot of work, and I spent many long hours in the library; However, I was determined to stick it out.

The fun times in college were attending hockey games, one basketball game, and going on a few dates. The UW Badgers had championship hockey teams those years, but poor football and basketball teams. One other fun time involved snow.

A few days before the fall semester break, I was up late studying for final exams. It started snowing outside— really heavy! Several other students in the dorms went outside to play football in the snow. One kid was from Georgia and had never seen snow before. I finally went to bed thinking of my exams the next day.

When I awoke the next morning, I turned on the radio. The school broadcast station was announcing that the entire campus was buried in over a foot of snow—the university was closed down and all classes were cancelled!

So, after breakfast, I decided to walk around campus, and headed to Bascom Hill, the centerpiece of the campus. To my surprise, a huge snowball fight was in progress. Two long lines of students stretched up and down the hill, about twenty feet apart. I joined in, enjoying throwing again, remembering my baseball days.

After about 30 minutes, everyone got tired and stopped throwing. Then several students started rolling large snow balls. Someone got the idea to create one very large snowball. When the snowball got to be about six feet in diameter, someone suggested that we push it down the hill. Bascom Hill is about one hundred yards down to the street. We got that big snowball rolling and down the hill it went. We were all cheering in amazement as we watched it hit the bottom of the hill, cross the sidewalk, and into the street. Then, by coincidence, a bus crossed its path—SLAM! That snowball hit the side of the bus. All the students let out one big WHOA! We then all scattered away, not wanting to wait around for campus police.

One classmate, Bob, was a horticulture major. He took me for a walk through the University Arboretum—I enjoyed that! He had a part-time job in his professor's research lab, and told me that they had an opening for a student lab technician. His professor agreed to hire me. So, on many Friday and Saturday nights, I worked in the Horticulture Lab running Kjeldahl chemical nitrogen analyses for protein content on peas. Then, during the summer, I also worked at the university research farm.

VISITING A DAIRY FARM

Bob had grown up on a real Wisconsin family dairy farm. I had never visited one, so, one weekend, we drove my Rambler about one hour north of Madison to his family farm for the weekend. It was an amazing experience.

Bob's parents were very welcoming. Bob had two younger brothers who still lived on the farm. The family meals were wonderful—fresh everything: eggs, unpasteurized whole milk, sweet corn-on-the-cob, fried chicken, mashed potatoes, real butter, vegetables, wild berries, and home-made ice cream. The farm house was very old with creaky wooden floors.

The next morning, a rooster woke us up at dawn. When we walked out of the house, chickens scurried across the yard. We then headed out into the farm pasture—many cows were scattered around, but not near us. I had, of course, seen many cows from a distance, but never up close. Bob and I were talking about the fresh air, beautiful scenery, and nice weather when suddenly I noticed that we were closely surrounded by cows! They are BIG animals!

I got nervous and asked Bob if we should run away, or what. He calmly said, "Just stay still. Cows are very friendly and curious." He suggested that I rub the top of their heads, between their ears. Suddenly, I felt a wet, sand-paper scrape up my arm—it was a cow's HUGE tongue! Whoa! It almost lifted me up off the ground.

Bob was laughing. I was freaking-out! However, I survived my first cow encounter. Bob then asked me if I wanted to try milking a cow. I declined.

We then took a hike to the back of the farm property, to the edge of the woods, and up a high hill—a moraine, formed by glacier activity over 10,000 years ago. At the top, we could see for miles—corn fields in every direction. I noticed that some fields had corn plants with white tassels on top; others had brown tassels.

"What is the difference?" I asked. Bob explained that sweet corn plants had the white tassels, while field corn, for cow silage, had the brown tassels.

Third THAT DAY

My third THAT DAY experience that significantly changed my life was actually a combination of three close events: a job offer, my graduation, and my first professional job.

The UW had an excellent placement office for graduating senior engineering students. The staff helped me create a job resume and set up on-campus employment interviews. I arranged for 13 interviews (I have always embraced that "unlucky" number), got three job offers, and took two interview trips. I accepted a position as a chemical process engineer in the corporate engineering division with a large chemical company near Philadelphia.

I actually graduated with a bachelor's degree of science (BS) in chemical engineering. What a relief! I was not the best student in my class, but I was confident that I had a sound theoretical education in chemistry, math, physics, thermodynamics, fluid mechanics, material and energy balances, material science, heat transfer, mass transfer, process flow diagrams, process controls, and process economics. I was ready to learn much-needed practical experience to try my effort at being a practicing engineer to design process systems, such as reaction systems, fluid transfers, piping systems, heat exchangers, distillations, and so on.

After graduation, I told Mom and Dad that I had accepted a job offer to work near Philadelphia.

They were surprised, and somewhat unhappy, that I was leaving Wisconsin. However, they were very supportive. I withdrew the remaining funds from my savings account—a $500 cashier's check. The morning that I was to leave home, before getting into my Rambler, Dad hugged me, wished me good luck, and told me to call home as soon as I got to my destination. Mom cried while standing by the washing machine, hugged me, kissed me and reminded me to write letters home frequently. At the age of 22, I was on my way to start my new life.

The first day at my new job, I was assigned to a senior engineer and his supervisor. I did not actually start working THAT DAY. Another young engineer was assigned to escort me around the area to look for an apartment. I had never lived in an apartment before. In school, I lived at home; then in the dorms and a fraternity house during summer.

After several visits, I chose one apartment. In the office, the manager told me that I needed to pay two month's rent up front (one for deposit). I pulled out my Wisconsin cashier's check for $500. The apartment manager laughed at me. He said that he could not accept a check from an out-of-state bank. That was my first experience in the financial side of life. What was I to do?

My escort engineer suggested that we return to the company office.

I walked into the division chief engineer's office and pleaded my dilemma. He said. "No problem." The company would issue a check for the apartment deposit and first month's rent. The money would be gradually deducted from my first six months' salary checks, without an interest charge. He suggested that I open a checking account at the local bank and deposit my cashier's check. I was relieved. This was a good company for me.

My first project was to help design an expansion for a distillation network of an impure, organic, acrylic monomer liquid mixture. The company produced several different monomers. In chemistry, a "monomer" is a liquid consisting of individual small organic molecules that can link up with each other to form a larger polymer chain or three-dimensional network solid in a process called polymerization.

My project was to refine the raw, impure monomer, and prevent polymerization. The refined monomer would later be polymerized in various processes to make a range of products, among them plexiglas glazing, molding powder, resins for water treatment, and emulsions for water-based paints. Acrylic molding powder consists of small, less-than-¼-inch sized, thermoplastic, solid cubes, used in injection molding of plastic parts. My project was to be installed at the company plant site located in Louisville, KY.

After completing the process design in the office, I wrote up process operating instructions, then visited the plant site to check out the equipment that other engineers had constructed, trained the process operators, and finally started up the process.

I next worked on a similar project for a plant site in Knoxville, TN. Then I became part of a large team to design a new chemical process plant for Fayetteville, NC, to produce polyester chips for making carpeting. I also worked on various processes at plant sites located in Bristol, PA; Philadelphia, PA; and Houston, TX,

Electronic technology was quickly advancing for our design efforts. The company had a mainframe computer for use with several prepared design programs. But we mainly used hand calculations with the aid of a slide rule. One day, my supervisor walked into my office with a novel device—a Hewlett-Packard handheld, scientific calculator. He demonstrated its use for quickly calculating products, quotients, powers, roots, and trigonometric functions that displayed numbers in tiny red, light-emitting diodes to eight digits—WOW!

"Guess how much it costs?" he asked.

We had no idea.

"$400!" he replied.

The company bought two calculators for us engineers to fight over.

The company also had active sports and social programs. My engineering division employees formed softball, basketball, volleyball, bowling, and tennis teams that played league matches with the nearby Bristol plant employees—great fun! I also went on several group downhill skiing trips. Learning how to snow ski after age 22 is not easy, but it was fun trying!

One day another employee walked into my office to ask me if I liked to go bowling. I responded that I had occasionally bowled for fun. He said that the division bowling team needed a substitute for the Friday night league. I agreed to try, but I acknowledged that I was just an average bowler.

That Friday night I arrived at the bowling alley, asked for a pair of shoes and searched for a house ball; the regular players all had their own private balls, bags, and shoes. I found a ball that seemed to fit my hand really well, but it was well-used with several nick marks. I met my team members—very welcoming people.

My first game felt amazing: surprisingly, I was not nervous though I did not want to embarrass myself. My body motion was very fluid, and I managed to achieve the best score of my life—240! My team members were astonished. They all said that I could substitute for them ANYTIME!

That's when I got nervous. What had I done? Could I possibly repeat such a feat? Not quite. My second game score was good, but not as spectacular—170. Then, the pressure was on. For the third game, I achieved a normal average score for me at 150. I felt disappointed, but the team members were very happy with my performance.

Could I become a good bowler? Another young engineer convinced me to go with him to the bowling alley to get fitted to buy a personal bowling ball, bag and shoes. We practiced. I occasionally substituted for the league team that season. Then, next season, I was invited to be a regular team member. I enjoyed the friendly fellowship of the league members. Unfortunately, I never quite achieved the success of that first night as a substitute. My regular average score was about 140. My bowling experience was similar to my experience in all sports—I would occasionally have terrific success, but it was very difficult for me to repeat those exceptional performances.

After a few months into my new life, I was lucky enough to get a first date: dinner and a movie. The movie was *Deliverance*—an adventure film about a canoe trip down a river with some archery scenes. I had read previews of the film in my *ARCHERY* magazine. My date said that she enjoyed the movie, but that she squirmed a bit in her seat during some of the scenes. It is one of my all-time favorite films. I had flashbacks to my fishing and hunting days with Dad and big brother Butchie.

At the end of the start-up project in Fayetteville, NC, I took a vacation to Hilton Head Island, SC, to attend a four-day tennis camp. It was a terrific experience. Not only did I improve my tennis skills, but I met one of the greatest professional tennis players of all time: Australian player ROD LAVER! I actually hit some warm-up rallies with him one morning. I noticed that he was hitting right-handed, but I thought that he was a lefty.

After our warm-ups, I was brave enough to question his hitting arm. He explained that he had "tennis elbow" pain in his left arm, and was no longer playing on the pro tour. He was a very soft-spoken, almost shy person. We were the same height. I have a beautiful autographed photo of us shaking hands.

JOB CHANGES

I worked for about seven years for that first company. I was still single when I was transferred to the Houston plant as a temporary technical service engineer. The job was interesting, and I was well-paid, but I felt uncomfortable working in the plant. Maybe I was a bit overwhelmed by the large plant size.

The first day in a chemical plant, new employees are given a short safety orientation, which included locating the windsock, which is located at the highest point in the plant-site. If an alarm sounds because of a large process leak, fire, or explosion, you should always look up at the windsock to determine the wind direction.

One time, a process valve failed wide-open, allowing a highly pressurized, flammable gas mixture to flow out through a safety flare stack, causing an explosion that almost destroyed the flare. A gas flare is a tall, slender

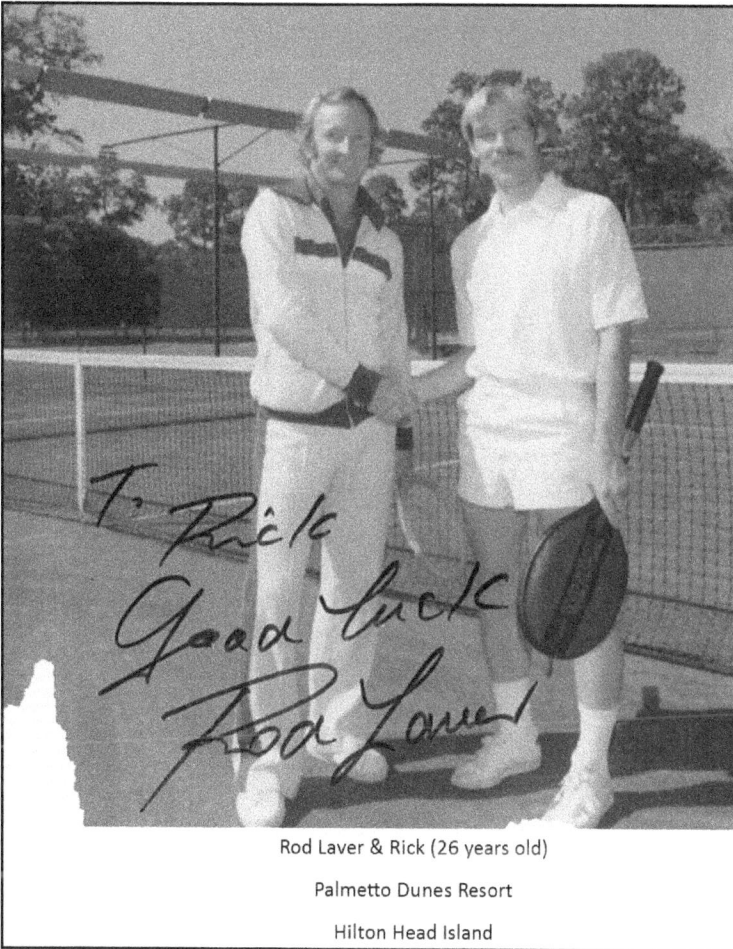

Rod Laver & Rick (26 years old)

Palmetto Dunes Resort

Hilton Head Island

stack with a pilot flame to burn-off process gases during upset conditions.

Then some process operators talked about the threat of a strike because of a contract dispute. Some older engineers and operators told me unsettling stories of past plant strikes. Also, my head and big ears were not compatible with wearing a hard hat every day. Nor did I like living in Houston, although I enjoyed attending baseball games with friends in the Astrodome, the world's first indoor sports stadium.

I decided to call a fellow engineer friend in Austin and asked if his company had any job openings. He said they did and arranged an interview for me. The company was an environmental contractor for the Federal government. I accepted their job offer, and moved to Austin, Texas. The job would only be temporary.

My single friend invited me to live with him in his three-bedroom house while I looked around the area for my own place to stay. There was no hurry, so I put my belongings in storage. About the third day at my new company, my supervisor walked into my office and asked if things were okay with my project.

"Yeah, sure", I replied. My project was to direct the development of air quality regulations for the client, the U.S. Environmental Protection Agency (EPA). He then said that he had another offer for me. He wanted me to move to Durham, NC with several other employees to open up a new branch office. The Durham branch office would be much closer to the government office. So, I moved with my new project to Durham, NC.

DURHAM, NC

Living and working in Durham turned out to be perfect for me and I flourished there. I became very involved in community activities. I joined and became an active volunteer in four non-profit organizations: a ski and sports club, the Eno River Association (ERA), Triangle Rails-to-Trails Conservancy (TRTC), and the Durham-Orange County Community Tennis Association (DOCTA).

Through the ski and sports club, I ventured into downhill and cross-country snow skiing, whitewater rafting, kayaking, canoeing, hiking, camping, beach trips, hang-gliding at Jockey's Ridge State Park on the Outer Banks, tennis leagues and tournaments; and many social gatherings. Special summer group outings included several historical plays performed outdoors, including *The Lost Colony* on Roanoke island; *The Sword of Peace* at Snow Camp; and *Unto These Hills* in Cherokee.

The ERA is an environmental land trust to protect the Eno River watershed from development along some 40 miles from its source in Hillsborough, through North Durham, to Falls Lake. The protected land has been established as the Eno River State Park. The ERA also offers on-going community stewardship and environmental education programs. Every 4th of July weekend, Durham hosts the trash-free (90+% recycling) "Festival for the Eno" as a fund-raiser event.

The TRTC was originally an advocate for preserving an abandoned railroad corridor that historically transported tobacco leaf from rural farms to the American Tobacco Company in Durham. When the company closed operations in Durham, there was no need for the railroad. TRTC then helped to create the Master Plan to convert the corridor to a commuter/recreational trail. TRTC was able to convince the NCDOT and the three counties of Chatham, Durham and Wake, to rail-bank the 22-mile long corridor, and to develop it to the current, very popular American Tobacco Rail-Trail.

DOCTA was formed to promote youth tennis on public courts. I had had little interaction with kids up to that time. For the first time in my life, I learned how to give back to community youth in leading group tennis lessons. When I was a kid, I had received lots of coaching from my Dad, and others, in baseball, but I had no experience helping others until then. Because of the success on the summer courts, I was recruited to coach a middle-school tennis team—girls, then boys. This was a real novel experience for me, but very rewarding.

Thanks to three office co-workers, I became an active bicyclist. I had not been on a bicycle since about age 14. My office co-workers were all from California, where road bicycling is popular among adults. They convinced me to try riding an extra bike that they had. We went for a short afternoon ride, which I enjoyed thoroughly. We then went on a weekend camping / riding trip. Great fun and I was hooked!

When I was 32 years old, Dad retired at age 63. I was working long hours at my job, and Dad (well deserved) could now partake in the good life. He enjoyed many fishing outings and two ocean cruises with Mom, went on hunting trips with friends, gardened, and picked berries with my Uncle Erv. I became jealous! About a year later, I requested a leave of absence from my employer to venture out on my first (of many) bicycle touring trips.

Before heading-out on the trip, I spent two weeks mapping-out my route, planning food supplies, bike maintenance and physical training. I went biking and running, and did stretching, and weights. My first bike tour was across eastern North Carolina, along the Outer Banks, and back to Durham. I enjoyed the solitude of biking on the back country roads, camping in state parks and on the beach, taking a ferry-boat ride across the Pamlico Sound, touring the lighthouses, walking up and down the high sand dunes at Jockey's Ridge State Park, visiting the Wright Brothers National Memorial at Kill Devil Hills and Museum at Kitty Hawk, and touring Elizabethan Gardens on Roanoke Island. The trip lasted about 15 days. I was not ready to return to work.

I notified my employer that I would not be returning to work and continued my leave of absence. I was planning another bike trip. My employer said okay, but they could not guarantee my job position past the 30-day leave of absence that I had initially been granted. I was willing to take the risk—I was single, had some savings, and had made some successful investments.

My second trip was a group ride and camping outing with the North Carolina Bicycle Touring Society. The route and campsites were already preplanned—I just had to enjoy the ride. The group ride included 15 people and was called "The Seven-Day Weekend." We met in High point, then, rode to Asheboro, and visited the North

Carolina Zoo. After that, we rode through Hillsborough, Chapel Hill, Madison, and back to High Point. What a great way to meet new friends!

My third bike trip was westward—by myself again—across the North Carolina Blue Ridge Mountains to Knoxville, Tennessee. That summer, there was a world's fair in Knoxville. Biking up and down the mountains was a lot more challenging than riding in the eastern flat lands of the state. I visited the fair for three days, staying in an air-conditioned dorm room on the University of Tennessee campus.

One day, on my return route, while riding on the Blue Ridge Parkway, I stopped at an inn to rest and refresh, and met several other bicyclists. One guy was from New Zealand, another from England. We swapped bicycling stories for over an hour.

The New Zealander and I were both headed east. So, we rode together for one day, and shared a campsite one night. He had been riding around Canada, Mexico, and Western U.S. for three years, stopping for a week or so at a time for part-time work. I really enjoyed his accent, which was different from English or Australian. This trip also lasted about 15 days.

Before returning to work, one of my bicycling co-workers asked me to join him on a trip to the Wilmington, NC area on the coast, for a stay at his family beach house. That trip took three days, one way. Another great ride.

I was now finally ready to return to work—for a few years.

One day, back in the office, my phone rang. It was Mom. Dad was in the hospital and had been diagnosed with colon cancer. I flew back to Wisconsin that night, and stayed with Mom about a week, until Dad recovered from surgery, and was released from the hospital.

About a year after that, my office phone rang again. This time it was Dad. Mom was in the hospital with heart disease. I flew back to Wisconsin that night, and stayed with Dad about a week, until Mom recovered from surgery, and was released from the hospital. Unfortunately, the stress on Dad was too great—he started smoking again. I did not try to stop him this time.

A few months after that, my office phone rang. It was Dad. Mom was in the hospital again with breast cancer and an aneurism. I flew back to Wisconsin that night. Mom had recovered from her surgeries, then lapsed into a coma. She was put on a ventilator. Dad would NOT leave the hospital; he paced between Mom's room and the nearby waiting room. He tried to sleep in the waiting room. I travelled back and forth between the house and the hospital with change of clothes, mail, and food for Dad.

Rose, my sister-in-law, visited the hospital several times. After 14 days, Mom passed away. She was 79 years old. Dad finally came home from the hospital. He slept in his bed for many hours while Rose helped me clean the house and make preparations for visitation by family and friends after the funeral. At the funeral, I was pleasantly surprised to meet my Uncle Frederick again. He was a religious man, and he wanted to pay his respects. Of course, Rose, Robbie, and Timmy (my two nephews) also attended.

At work, computer technology was just becoming available for office use. The secretaries had computerized typewriters with floppy-disk memory storage. Our office had one desktop IBM PC. A lot of schools were given McIntosh personal computers by the Apple Computer Company. Some people were buying one or the other of the computers for home use.

As part of my engineering studies in college, I had a two-week session on Fortran language for the IBM mainframe computer; However, I had no knowledge or skills regarding either of the desktop computers. I had read several newspaper articles about developing semi-conductor technology and computer chips. I also saw an advertisement for computer classes at the local community college. I was curious to learn more.

I decided to visit Durham Technical Community College to register for an introductory computer class. After the first class, I talked with the instructor for a while. He convinced me to quit my job and to enroll in the full, two-year Microelectronics curriculum. While in college again, I worked part-time as a peer tutor in chemistry, math, and electronics. I learned how to use the Apple McIntosh and IBM-PC computers, and I learned the software language, PASCAL.

A requirement in the curriculum was a psychology course called "Interpersonal Communications," which was very enlightening for me! One assignment was to write an essay regarding our personal views on the three personality traits: child, parent, and adult. I explained that my personality was dominated mostly by the child trait (I liked to play), and enough of an adult trait to manage my life and work, but almost no parent traits (never married, and had no children).

Another time the instructor asked the students to verbally describe their personalities in one word. I chose "Punctual." Dad had always told me to be on time for appointments and meetings; My engineering college placement advisors counseled me to always be early for interviews.

During the last semester of the program, one instructor helped me get a part-time job as a clean-room technician at the Microelectronics Center of North Carolina, in Research Triangle Park, just a few miles from Durham. Wearing the "bunny suits" while in the clean room and learning hands-on how computer chips, consisting of many integrated circuits, are fabricated on thin silicon wafers, was interesting and challenging.

I completed the curriculum and earned an associate degree in applied science (AAS) for Microelectronics. However, the Center had no permanent job openings for me. One of my instructors offered to set up an interview with a technology company in Texas, but I declined—I wanted to stay in North Carolina. So, I began a job search. I wondered if I should go back to my previous company?

I responded to a job advertisement in the newspaper for an environmental permitting engineer at a local company that had just spun-off from a larger engineering construction firm. I interviewed for the job and accepted the offer. I was back at work, but not in microelectronics.

My new projects involved directing the application for air quality operating permits, and assessing process safety management for industrial clients. I also managed the operation and maintenance for a client's groundwater remediation system, and sometimes assisted other water quality engineers in sampling groundwater monitoring wells. I learned, on the job, how to use computer spreadsheets, word processing programs, and EPA-issued air dispersion modeling programs for air pollution assessments.

Then I bought an Apple McIntosh personal computer and a dot-matrix printer for my home use. I used MacDraw and MacPaint applications to create bicycling route maps; CricketGraph to track financial records; MacWrite for letters and documents; and the Reflex database to maintain membership records and to printout mailing labels for the ski and sports club.

While I lived in Durham, I met a river and trail guide, "River Dave." In the warm weather months, he led group trips on the Eno River in his inflatable, two-person rubber boats. In the colder months, he led group hiking trips around the area. He also arranged group trips to Central and South America during the winter months. He convinced me to go with him to Costa Rica for ten days.

Costa Rica offered great scenery; amazing strangler fig trees; lots of strange wild flowers; howler monkeys; poisonous tree frogs; macaws, resplendent quetzals, hummingbirds, toucans, and other birds; and a wide variety of tropical fruits.

I lived in Durham for about 20 years. I made a lot of friends, and had several opportunities for female companionship; However, I never had any desire to marry, raise children, or do that "family thing." Mom and Dad drove from Wisconsin to visit me where I was working at several locations: Bristol, Fayetteville, Houston, and Durham. I routinely visited Mom and Dad in Wisconsin during Christmas vacations, and sometimes during summer fishing trips. I visited old school friends, as well as Rose, Rob, and Tim. However, there was no contact with brother Ron.

After Mom died, Dad started writing letters to me—unusual for him. Over about ten years, he sent 15 hand-written letters and I have saved every one.

He drove from Wisconsin to visit me in Durham that first Christmas after Mom passed away. He was trying to quit smoking. He was really lonely. However, his life would change for the better in about a year.

Chapter 10
DAD'S SINGLE LIFE

AFTER MOM DIED, DAD STRUGGLED emotionally. They had been married for 43 years. Dad did have a companion though—a house dog, a pug, named "Muggs." Muggs was really Mom's pet, but now Dad clung to that little critter.

Dad enjoyed letting Muggs sit on his lap while he sat in his big lounge chair watching TV, or reading a book, newspaper, or magazine. Dad always had the radio playing to a sports talk show. Dad also let Muggs sit in his lap in the car. I suggested to Dad that that was hazardous to his driving, but Dad ignored me; I did not press the issue. I visited Dad in Wisconsin every Christmas holiday.

As I mentioned, Dad started writing letters to me. Mom and I had exchanged letters over the years, but never Dad. In one letter, he enclosed a newspaper article with a photograph of him volunteer working in a Toys-for-Tots, non-profit workshop, repairing kids bicycles. I told him that seemed to be perfect for him.

He also frequently visited his sister, my Aunt Louise, and Uncle Erv, in Waukesha. During the summer, they went berry-picking at their property in Northern Wisconsin. Dad also wrote about his wonderful neighbors who baked goodies for him and visited him frequently.

Then, about a year after Mom passed away, Dad sent me a very happy letter.

HARRIET

In early December, Dad sent me a letter telling me that he had met a lady named Harriet. He wanted me to meet her when I visited at Christmas holiday. He asked if that was okay with me. After reading the entire letter, I called Dad.

"Absolutely, yes!" I told him.

He sounded so happy on the phone. Dad was now about 70 years old.

During my Christmas visit, I met Harriet. They explained to me their courtship. Dad had had his hair cut by the same barber forever—Roy. By coincidence, Roy lost his wife about the same time as Dad did. Roy hosted a backyard cookout party for his customers, friends and neighbors. Dad and Harriet met at that party.

Harriet had also recently lost her husband. Dad was impressed with her; however, Harriet said that she thought he was nice, but no special feelings: Dad was a country boy and she was a city girl—not compatible, no match?

The next day, Dad got Harriet's phone number from Roy, and called her. Harriet was surprised at Dad's call, but enjoyed talking with him. Dad suggested they take a car drive in the country. Harriet was hesitant, but agreed

"What else did I have to do?" she told me.

During their outing, they stopped by a lake and fed some ducks. Then they had dinner at a country inn.

"It was a wonderful date," Harriet said.

They began to see each other frequently.

The second day that I visited Harriet, Dad was outside shoveling snow off her driveway. He enjoyed that. Harriet and I were in her kitchen, preparing dinner. She told me how much she loved Dad, and how much fun they enjoyed together.

Then she shocked me. She said that she did not want to have sex with Dad, and did not want to marry him. I almost fell down. Why had she shared that with me? I just relied, "Okay."

Dad and Harriet took several Elder Hostel trips together around the country. Elder Hostels offer group outings geared for an older population that may be on a more limited or fixed budget. Travelers stay in down-to-earth locations like college campuses and YMCAs. One outing was to Glacier National Park in Montana. I did not even know there was such a place.

Dad and Harriet enjoyed about ten years together.

Over the next several years, Dad's health slowly declined. When Dad got colon cancer, his surgery removed one-third of the organ (ascending part). The doctor told me that the cause was uncertain, but a history of smoking and a high-fat, low-fiber diet probably contributed. Dad recovered okay from the surgery, but never altered his eating habits. So, when Mother Nature called him, you did not want to stand in his way—he had to run to the bathroom (with only two-thirds of a colon).

Then, he got COPD (chronic obstructive pulmonary disease), again from smoking, that complicated his history of asthma. His doctor prescribed medicated inhalers, and an oxygen generator machine for the house, with a long plastic breathing tube that stretched throughout the house. Dad also started getting regular deliveries of pressurized, bottled oxygen to take with him in the car. Even with all of those health problems, he was enjoying his life with Harriet.

Fourth THAT DAY

I was maybe 45 years old, still single and living in Durham, when I had my fourth THAT DAY experience that significantly changed my life.

My phone rang. "Rick, this is Janet.".

"Janet who?" I asked.

I did not know anyone named Janet, I thought.

"Your sister Janet in Racine, dummy!"

I was really surprised and confused. I had never talked on the phone with her, and had not even talked with her for many years. She had gotten my phone number and address from our brother Ron. She told me that she had two children who wanted to meet their Uncle Rick. Was I ever planning to get back to Racine? I said that I would be visiting Dad over the Christmas holiday. Janet told me that the rest of our biological family still lived in Racine. She would try to arrange a holiday reunion. She gave me her phone number so I could call her when I returned to Wisconsin. I was impressed with her plans, but not really expecting much of a result.

While visiting Dad at Christmas, I called Janet. She said that her family reunion plans had changed. She could not convince all of our family members to meet at once. So, our new agenda was for us to drive around Racine to visit each family member, individually. I drove Dad's car to Janet's house.

When she opened the door, I did not recognize her—she looked different from one childhood photo that I had seen. We enjoyed a warm embrace. I met her sons—my two nephews. After that, our first visit was to Uncle Frederick and his wife.

Janet and I climbed into my car. She immediately pulled out a cigarette and started to light it. I stopped her.

"You smoke?" I asked. "You are not smoking in my car!" I ordered.

"Rick, I have to smoke, or I will get the shakes," she replied.

"How far is it to Uncle Frederick's house?" I asked.

"Not far, maybe ten minutes," she said. "Hold off on smoking until we get there," I said.

"Ok, I will try," she said.

When we arrived at Uncle Frederick's house, Janet jumped out of the car, immediately lit-up a cigarette, and practically swallowed it. I was astonished. She was so addicted. After she finished her smoke, we rang the doorbell.

We visited for about an hour. I thoroughly enjoyed re-connecting with Uncle Frederick and meeting his wife. Janet was squirming in her seat and started poking me that we needed to leave. Once we got out of the house, Janet again immediately lit-up a cigarette and again practically inhaled it.

Back in the car, we headed to our next destination— brother Ron. After about 20 minutes, we were on the correct street and looking for house addresses. Then we saw Ron out walking his dogs in his driveway. He waved at us, and yelled, "Over here, you two dummies!"

Janet jumped out of the car and gave Ron a big hug. Then she pulled out a cigarette and walked into the house. Janet knew that Ron's wife also smoked. Ron did not smoke. I do not know how he could live with a smoker! Ron and I sat near each other; Janet and Ron's wife puffed away near each other, very content.

It was great to see my big brother Butchie again. Ron reminisced a bit about living with me as kids in Crestview, and how difficult Mom was to live with. He also explained that he had back surgery, and was on disability from a back injury while at his sheet metal work.

Janet was in no hurry to leave this time. She was enjoying the smoking session. However, we finally left for our next visit.

Our sister Kathy lived with her boyfriend in Union Grove, just a few miles from Racine. They lived in a very nice double-wide trailer. I had never really met Kathy (not since I was three years old). She was short, with a beautiful smile, a happy face, and a very pleasant personality. Kathy's husband had died many years ago when they owned a horse farm.

Our next visit was to St. Mary's Hospital, where our sister Marlene worked as an emergency room nurse. Again, I hadn't seen Marlene since I was three years old. She asked a lot of questions about our lives. It felt weird talking with my sister, who really was a stranger.

Then, our final visit was to sister Jackie's house. I recognized Jackie, since I had seen her at Ron and Rose's wedding. Jackie introduced us to her six children. Again, Janet really enjoyed this visit since Jackie was also a smoker. They lit it up as we sat around the kitchen table.

After a while, our brother Allen walked into the house—it was great to see him! Allen reminded me that he had changed his name to Tom. He also was a smoker. So there I was, reminiscing with two long-lost sisters and a brother, while sucking-in secondhand cigarette smoke— talk about mixed emotions!

THE MOVE BACK TO RACINE

Several years later, my last Christmas visit to Dad was difficult and filled with mixed emotions. Dad's health problems were getting worse. In addition to his complications from colon cancer, asthma and COPD, he had congestive heart failure (CHF) and edema in both legs. His legs had swelled up from lack of proper blood circulation. The poor guy was a mess! However, he was surviving on inhaler medication, the oxygen generator machine, and a boat-load of drugs. Fortunately, Dad's brain still functioned well, and he still had a very friendly personality.

Unfortunately, Dad's friend Harriet got dementia. She sometimes did not recognize Dad's voice over the phone when he called her. Harriet's son had moved her into an assisted living facility. We visited her together one time. Of course, Dad was sad for Harriet. They had enjoyed almost ten years together.

Before I returned to Durham, Dad and I agreed that I would move back to Racine to help him. Dad was over-joyed at my decision. However, I needed some time to quit my job and finish my middle-school team tennis coaching season. So, we planned for me to move back by May first.

In Durham, I prepared for my move back to Wisconsin. I quit my job and ended my tennis coaching duties. I said goodbye to friends and made arrangements for others to assume my volunteer duties in the four non-profit organizations that I enjoyed.

My tennis friends threw me a going-away party. I hired a moving van to transport my furniture and bicycle back to Racine. I packed-up my car with clothes and necessities. I was sad to leave Durham, but happy that I had decided to help Dad.

At age 48, I drove back to "home" to Racine. It was a Friday when I arrived at the Crestview house. I noticed that Dad's car was not in the garage. When I started to unload the stuff from my car into the house, I noticed the door was not locked—as usual.

After a few minutes, Dad's car pulled into the driveway. However, Dad was not driving. A neighbor had taken Dad for a doctor visit. I walked to the passenger side of the car, opened the car door, and greeted Dad. He was not happy. He barked at me to help him out of the car and to get into the house. When we arrived at the back door, I walked through first, then turned around to help pull Dad in. However, he was stuck. He grumbled at me that he could not move. I could not see what the problem was. I suggested that he back up, and try again. He was having trouble lifting his foot up high enough to clear the door step. We finally managed to get Dad into the house and seat him in his big lounge chair. He had difficulty breathing, even with the breathing tube and the oxygen machine. He was miserable.

At that moment, it hit me. I was now a caretaker for my elder Dad. I had no experience in this since I had never married and no children. Could I handle it?

The neighbor who had driven Dad's car explained to me about the doctor visit. Dad was to take some new medication over the weekend. On Monday, I was to call the doctor.

Dad had a miserable weekend. He could not sleep lying down in bed and tried to sleep in his lounge chair. The new medication did not help his problems. Monday morning, I called the doctor's office. I asked for an immediate appointment.

The doctor examined Dad and decided to admit him to St. Mary's Hospital. Dad had several problems: complications from colon cancer, COPD, edema in his legs, and congestive heart failure. In other words, he was a mess.

DAD IN HOSPITAL

I sensed that Dad had only a few days left and called several people to notify them that Dad was in the hospital. Rose, Rob, and Tim visited. Dad's neighbors visited. One retired work friend visited. My Uncle Erv and Aunt Louise (Dad's sister) from Waukesha visited. Harriet and her son visited.

Who else might want to see Dad?

I thought of my big brother Butchie. I had not contacted him for many years. So, I looked up his name in the phone book—there it was. I called Ron. When he visited Dad in the hospital, Ron and I hugged. I cried uncontrollably, like a little kid. It was great to see my big brother Butchie again! He was still taller than me—I was about 5 ft. 8 in. and Ron was over 6 feet tall. Ron said that he was caring for his father (our biological father) as well. I had no memory of our father.

I talked with Dad's pulmonary doctor. He said that Dad should not be living alone once he got out of the hospital. He suggested assisted living. I questioned the doctor about COPD. He said that the entire hospital floor was filled with COPD patients from smoking habits. He could not predict how long Dad had to live.

Thus, my new life meant traveling back and forth between the house and the hospital. I did maintenance on the house and yard. I took Dad's mail to him. He would look it over and give me instructions to pay bills, house maintenance, and so on.

Dad's mind was still sharp and alert. However, after about ten days, Dad grew really frustrated at being in the hospital. He told me to stop bringing mail to him. Dad had prepared documents for me to be his healthcare provider, financial power of attorney, and his only heir in his will. He was satisfied with my handling all affairs, except one.

Dad's car was really messy inside—newspapers and clothing scattered. So, I decided to clean it up, inside and outside — remove the newspapers and clothing. I told Dad that I had cleaned-up his car, which was a really bad idea! He barked at me that he needed those newspapers and clothing in the car because he frequently had bowel control problems. I ended up replacing a few newspapers in the car.

Slowly, Dad was recovering. His edema went away and his breathing was much better.

After 25 days, the doctor assigned physical therapy for Dad to prepare him to leave the hospital. Harriet and her son visited Dad. Harriet suggested that Dad move into the same assisted living facility with her. Dad then told me to go to the facility and get information on availability and cost.

I started a search for Dad's new home. I visited Harriet's assisted living facility. They had a room available for Dad. They quoted me three cost structures based on level of care. I then searched through all of Dad's financial records, and completed an income statement. Dad had just enough income from savings, Social Security, work pension, and some stock dividends, and bond interest to cover even the highest level of care.

I presented my report to Dad.

"You can do it!" I said.

He did not believe that he had that much income. "Where did I get that much money?" he asked.

I replied that he and Mom had been very frugal and wisely invested some savings. He told me to redo the income statement—I must have made a mistake. So, I returned to Dad's house, re-evaluated his financial records, and came up with the same result. Dad finally accepted my report. We notified Harriet that Dad would be moving to her facility. Dad was happy again.

DAD AT ASSISTED LIVING

Finally, in July, Dad was well enough to leave the hospital. I moved him into the assisted living facility where Harriet stayed. They each had separate rooms. Dad had laundry service, bathroom cleaning service, three daily meals served, and nursing care for his medications. I breathed a sigh of relief—he was in good hands.

Unfortunately, Dad did not like the facility at first. He did not make new friends easily, and Harriet with her dementia did not visit with Dad much. One time, when I visited Dad, we searched for Harriet, and saw her sitting in the lounge area with another man—holding hands. Of course, that made Dad very sad, but he told me that he understood.

Dad eventually grew more comfortable in his new home. The staff were terrific. He made a few new friends to play card games and chess. I called several people to notify that Dad was at assisted living. Rose, Rob, and Tim visited. Dad's neighbors visited. My Uncle Erv and Aunt Louise (Dad's sister) from Waukesha visited. He started to take daily walks outside with a wheeled walker for exercise, short walks at first then longer each day. Finally, he was able to walk all the way around the facility.

"I am back!" he exclaimed to me.

I visited him several times each week to watch sports on his TV or go for a drive in the country. I set up a cash account for him at the facility. His retired work friend would sometimes pick up Dad for lunch, but Dad would insist on paying the bill.

I asked Dad if he wanted to see anyone.

"No," he said.

"Would you like to see Ron?" I suggested.

"Yes," he replied. So, I called my brother Butchie and asked if he would visit my Dad in assisted living. Ron agreed and visited Dad. Unfortunately, I was at work during the visit and missed Butchie.

After getting Dad settled in assisted living, I decided that I did not want to live in the Crestview house. I was surprised at how much the community had expanded. It had taken-over adjacent farm fields. The old sand pits were gone, covered over by new houses. My old baseball field was covered over with commercial businesses.

I moved out of the house and into an apartment in Racine. Rose and Rob helped me. I then contacted a realtor to sell the house. The realtor decided to advertise the house as "a fixer-upper" sale. An inspection report showed several problems: electrical and plumbing systems were no longer to code, the fireplace brickwork was crumbling, roof shingles needed replacement, some foundation supports needed replacement, and several wooden boards on the garage were rotted and needed replacement.

Another problem for Wisconsin — the house was only partially insulated. However, the yard was attractive. The house and property sold for $50,000. Dad and I discussed what to do with the proceeds from the house sale. We decided to invest it in a dividend investment fund to help pay Dad's living expenses

Next, I decided that I could start looking for employment. One day, I took Dad's car for service: four new tires and tune-up. The service shop offered a shuttle van ride back to Dad's assisted living facility. During the van ride, I asked the driver how long he had been driving the shuttle. He said since he had retired from his regular job. He enjoyed it. He then asked me what I did. I replied that I was caring for my Dad, and I was starting to look for a job—maybe part-time.

He asked if I had a college degree. I said yes. He then told me that the public schools needed a lot of substitute teachers. He explained that the State had negotiated a new teacher's contract, allowing teachers more personal business days. Also, the State now allowed anyone with any college degree to substitute teach. Maybe, I should check on that as a part-time job.

Substitute Teacher and Tutor

I visited the Racine Unified Public Schools administration office, and filled out an application for substitute teaching. I preferred math and science classes in high schools. They offered a one-day training session. Then, I paid a $100 fee for a three-year substitute teaching license. I was told that a computerized system would call me when jobs became available. During the second week after school started in September, I stated receiving phone messages on my answering machine—multiple substitute teaching jobs every week!

My first day at substitute teaching was quite eventful. The job was for a Friday in Special Education at my old high school. I did not know what that involved, but I was intrigued to be at my old school. So, I dressed in my gray suit (all male teachers dressed in suits when I was in school), carried my briefcase, and reported to the school office at 6:45 am. I was filled with nostalgia as I walked through the school halls.

At the office, one staff person was talking on the phone. I waited. Finally, I was able to get her attention, and explained that I was a first-time substitute teacher. She grumbled at me, told me to find my teacher's mail box, to collect the attendance sheets, and to report to the teacher's office.

When I got to the Special Education office, no one was there. I walked around looking on each desk for my teacher's name or a note to me — nothing. What should I do? Fortunately, a few minutes later, the department chair entered the office and greeted me. He had no idea what my teacher had planned for me to do with her classes that day. No agenda sheet had been placed on the desk. He then gave me a stack of *Weekly Reader* magazines, and suggested that I pass them out to students, then assign reading parts for a story in the magazine.

The bell rang for my first class. The room was on the other side of the large building, in the balcony of the old boys' gym. The balcony had been partitioned off to form several small classrooms. I walked into the room to find only one student sitting at a small table. He was working on a word-search puzzle.

I introduced myself, and sat next to him. No response. So, I just remained quiet and watched him work the puzzle. A few minutes later, another teacher walked into the room. He introduced himself, and said that he had the class in the next room. He explained that only the one student would be in this class today.

About three-quarters of the way through the period, my student jumped-up out of his chair, and said, "I have had enough of this shit!", and ran out of the room. I tried to follow him, then I shouted, "Help, I have lost my student!"

The teacher in the next room told me to sit with his class, and he would run after my student. So, I sat with his ten students, who were giggling at me until the bell rang for the next period. I do not know what happened with my "lost" student.

Second period was even more eventful. My next class was also in one of the nearby balcony classrooms. This class had 20-some students. So, I handed-out the *Weekly Reader* magazines, and asked the students who wanted to read parts in the story. The students began reading. All seemed okay—until I turned my back. I faced the green chalk board to write out questions for the students to answer after completing the story. Then I heard giggling.

When I turned around, I noticed that the large clock on the wall had been advanced to read a time near the end of the period!

I said, "Whoever advanced the clock, please reset it to the correct time." So, a student jumped up, and walked toward the clock. I then turned back around to face the green chalk board—bad idea. A few seconds later, I heard a loud crash. I turned around to see that the clock had fallen off of the wall and smashed on the floor.

Suddenly, the classroom door opened. A teacher from the adjacent room ran in, and shouted, "What is going on in here?" I pointed to the smashed clock on the floor. Of course, the entire class of students were laughing hysterically. Finally, the bell rang for the next period.

My third period had four students in a small room. One student grabbed a chair and sat in it facing a corner of the room the entire period. The other students suggested that I not bother him; he did that some days. The other three students read the reader story okay.

Fourth period had about 20 students. They read the reader story okay, except for one student who liked to occasionally swear out loud. I asked him if he could please hold it down. The others students laughed, but he did calm down. I do not remember the remainder of my first day at substitute teaching, but I was questioning my decision at the job.

I also noticed that none of the male teachers wore suits, and many students wore blue jeans—the dress code for both teachers and students was much more lenient than when I had been in school.

After school that day, I visited Dad. I regurgitated for him my first school experience as a substitute teacher. He was astonished. I suggested that I should not accept any more "Special Education" assignments, and I should not wear a suit. Dad agreed. He was happy, though, that I was working again.

The following week, I accepted my second substitute teaching assignment—math classes. I was pleasantly surprised when I walked into the math office to find a complete daily agenda sheet on my teacher's desk. Five math classes: two geometry, two algebra II / trigonometry, and one pre-calculus. In each class, after a short lecture, I walked up and down the student rows offering to help students with problems.

They all seemed to appreciate that effort on my part. Most regular teachers are too busy to do that. In one class, one student asked me if I would consider tutoring her at home. I gave her my phone number, and told her to have her parents call me. I did start tutoring that student, and started a tutoring business—meeting students at their home, parent's work office, or public library.

Rose's Mom

At my new apartment one day, I was at the hall mail boxes checking my mail. An elderly lady walked out of her apartment to see if she had mail. We looked at each other. Did we know each other? She looked familiar.

I introduced myself. Her eyes opened wide, and she shouted, "Rick, I am Rose's Mom!" We hugged.

I had only met her a few times, many years ago. Her husband had died several years ago. She now lived alone. We started visiting each other occasionally. She baked some goodies for me. I called Rose to tell her that I had met her mom. Rose liked that. Rose's mom shared with me a few stories.

One story involved her family and my biological family. She confirmed that the two families were close friends. However, she did not like that her husband and my biological father were drinking buddies. One time, late at night, her four girls in the family were all in bed sleeping, and her husband was out somewhere with my biological father. Then, her husband's car pulled into the driveway. Four people stumbled out of the car: her husband, my biological father, another man, and my biological mother—all drunk. They staggered into the house, and spent the night sleeping on the floor in the living room.

(My sister Marlene told me NOT to believe this story. Marlene had asked Father about this and other similar stories. Father denied all of the stories.)

DAD'S LAST DAYS

Dad's health problems progressed. During September and October, Dad was in and out of the hospital several times. Each hospital stay was a few days. Then, in early November, the hospital stay was final. Dad was on morphine, sleeping most of the time, and occasionally waking to ask me, "Are you still here?"

One evening, I had gone home to get some sleep. Rose, Rob, and Tim were visiting Dad. Rob later told me that he was holding Dad's hand when Dad suddenly gasped for a deep breath, and died.

When I got back to the hospital, a lady from hospice was in the room. She was wonderful at consoling me and suggesting that I call the funeral home.

Dad died on November 12. He was 79 years old; I was 49.

What to do now?

The next day, Rose accompanied me to the funeral home to make funeral arrangements and to submit an obituary for the newspaper. I then went to Dad's bank. We had already reassigned the checking account as joint in both our names. I closed-out Dad's safety deposit box, which contained a copy of his will, power of attorney, the original deed to the Crestview property, the original mortgage notes, and the original layout diagram for roads and lots for the Crestview Subdivision.

I next went to the River Bend Nature Center to make a donation in Dad's name, and to request that a memorial bench seat with Dad's name on it be installed near the big pond. The following day, I went to the county court house to file for probate. I spent the next several months filing legal documents, including Dad's final tax return.

Did I want to stay in Wisconsin or move back to Durham, NC?

Mark Hertzberg/Journal Times *Nov. 1990*

Santa's helper

Dozens of volunteers are busy fixing toys for the annual Tex Reynolds Toys for Tots program. Clarence Burt played Santa's helper while fixing a bicycle for the drive. Toys will be handed out the weeks of Nov. 26 and Dec. 3. Last year 1,336 families with 3,306 children were served.

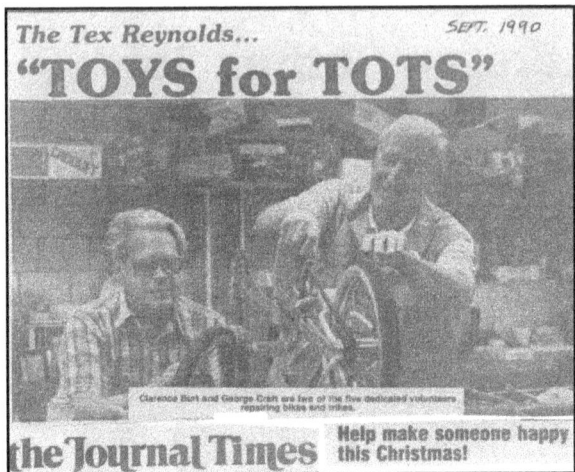

The Tex Reynolds...   *SEPT. 1990*

"TOYS for TOTS"

Clarence Burt and George Craft are two of the five dedicated volunteers repairing bikes and trikes.

the Journal Times   **Help make someone happy this Christmas!**

Chapter 11

LATER YEARS AND
RECONNECTION

AFTER SETTLING DAD'S ESTATE, I decided to stay in Wisconsin for a few years. I was enjoying helping students at my academic tutoring business. Substitute teaching was interesting, as long as I stayed away from special education classes. In addition, the school system hired me to help administer the federally mandated computerized testing program to comply with the Federal "No Child Left Behind Program."

When not working, I started enjoying my hobbies again—tennis, bicycling, hiking, going to the beach, and volunteering. I re-connected with some old school friends. I also decided to fulfill three childhood wishes:

1) Revisit the Chicago Museum of Science and Industry,

2) Re-visit the Racine Heritage Museum, and

3) Visit the town of Prairie Du Chien.

I began volunteering at community events and organizations: River Bend Nature Center, triathlon races (swim, bike and run) along the lake front, bike races in downtown Racine, running events, gift wrapping at the Regency Mall during the Christmas holidays, and decoration setups / takedowns at the zoo for Christmas. I also became an active member in two non-profit organizations: Sustainable Racine and Bright Public Power.

Sustainable Racine was established by the SC Johnson Company to help invigorate the community. It had several volunteer committees. One to encourage planting trees and gardens. I served on the energy committee to promote the use of more insulation in buildings and installation of solar systems to generate electricity and for water heating.

Bright Public Power was set up by a member of Racine's City Council as a response to Wisconsin Energy's proposal to expand a local coal-fired power plant. The mission was to bring a non-profit, community-owned, public electric utility that would provide safe, reliable, and environmentally responsible energy to the Greater Racine area, at a lower cost. Unfortunately, the coal-fired plant expansion was completed, greatly increasing railcar traffic through Racine.

I re-visited the two museums of my childhood memories. I walked to the Racine Heritage Museum— great displays of the city's industrial and commercial fishing past. I also researched some family and neighborhood information in the archives room. I rode the commuter train from the Kenosha station to Chicago three times—novel for me.

Chicago is a BIG city! I felt overwhelmed walking from the train station to the museum, but it was a very satisfying adventure. The Museum of Science and Industry is terrific—a kid's (and my) wonderland.

I walked on the nearby rail-trail several days a week, and I was back on my bicycle again. On weekends, I rode my bicycle along the rail-trail path between Racine and Kenosha, and along the lakeshore paths. I frequently stopped at the West Lawn Cemetery to visit several family graves:

- Ruth and Clarence Burt (my adoptive parents);
- Charles Richard Winsall (Ron and Rose's infant son),
- Dorothy Anders (my biological mother);
- Judy Nelson (my biological sister);
- Johanna and Louis Niebergall (my biological grandparents); and
- Louis Frederick Niebergall (my biological uncle).

I lost Uncle Frederick when I was 54; he was 80 years old when he died. One day, I bicycled along the Racine city street where my biological family lived. I located the addresses for the two houses that belonged to my family and my grandparents. I stopped by each house for a few minutes, and thought of knocking on the doors. However, I decided not to—the emotion might be overwhelming.

Several times I also biked to Cliffside County Park near the Crestview Subdivision, walked through the old woods and the ravine to the lake bluff, and walked around my old elementary school grounds (now a Catholic church)—many memories. I did not bicycle along Paul Bunyan Road, my childhood street—again to prevent overwhelming emotion.

WISCONSIN BIKE TOUR

In grade school, I had read an interesting story involving the town of Prairie du Chien. I thought that someday I should visit there. So, I decided to take another bike tour, this time around Wisconsin, destination Prairie du Chien.

Prairie du Chien is a small town of about 5,000 people, located just above the confluence of the Mississippi and Wisconsin rivers, in the southwestern part of the state. The word *chien* is French for "dog." The town was established by French traders during the 1600s, and is the second oldest state city after Green Bay.

The state is famous for establishing the first rail-trail bicycle path in the United States: the Elroy-Sparta State Trail. A rail-trail is a hiking/biking trail converted from an abandoned rail corridor, that has been rail-banked by the state. Sparta, with about 8,000 residents, is the self-proclaimed "Bicycling Capital of America."

So, I planned a route from Racine westward along county roads for 140 miles, around Madison, the state capitol, through Sun Prairie to Lake Wisconsin (a wide portion in the Wisconsin River). There, I crossed the lake on a free car ferry (no road bridge). A few miles down the road, I camped at Devils Lake State Park (an amazing creation of long-ago glacial activity).

Then, it was ten more miles to the city of Reedsburg. There, I rode onto the 400 State Trail for 22 miles to Elroy. Then I rode on the Elroy-Sparta State Trail for 32 miles, including three old train tunnels, on my way to Sparta.

Next, I connected to the La Crosse River State Trail for 22 miles to La Crosse, on the Mississippi River. From there, I travelled north along the big river for about 15 miles to Perrot State Park. I returned south along the river, through La Crosse, to Goose Island State Park. There, I rented a kayak for a few hours to paddle on the Mississippi River and adjacent wetlands.

Finally I arrived in Prairie du Chien. I toured old Fort Crawford Museum. Then I biked across the river to Iowa and Pikes Peak State Park, at an elevation of about 500 feet above the river. This offered a great view of the confluence of the Wisconsin River with the Mississippi River. The park is named after the explorer Zebulon Pike, who also named a park in Colorado.

My return ride to Racine started eastward, following the south side of the Wisconsin River for a few miles, then south to Governor Dodge State Park. From there, I rode onto the Military Ridge State Trail for 40 miles to Madison. I biked along Lake Mendota to the University of Wisconsin campus, and right past my old dormitory, where I stopped for a few minutes to reminisce. Then, I continued along the lake path to the Memorial Student Union. Again, I stopped for a few minutes to reminisce.

I crossed through the city to Lake Monona, where I got onto that bike path and rode eastward for nine miles to Cottage Grove. There, I rode onto the Glacial Drumlin State Rail-Trail for 52 miles to Waukesha. I stopped at a public phone booth to call my Uncle Erv and Aunt Louise. They let (or made) me shower at their house, and then we went out for dinner. I camped in their back yard. The next day, I rode home to Racine. The trip lasted 12 days.

Fifth THAT DAY

The fifth THAT DAY that significantly changed my life was when I attended my nephew Rob's wedding reception. He is my brother Ron's oldest son.

Rob had married for the first time at age 39 (I was 57). When I walked into the Kenosha Country Club, I waited in the guest line. Finally, at the front of the line, my brother Ron greeted me—we hugged. It was great to see my brother again. He was a proud dad. It had been nine years since Ron visited my Dad and me. We did not talk, as he had a long line of guests to greet.

I then walked into the reception hall, and greeted Rob and his new bride with my wedding gift. After that, I walked around to find my assigned seat at the dining tables. There, I met my older sister Marlene and younger sister Janet. It had been about 13 years since our Christmas reunion. I really enjoyed reminiscing with them.

After we finished the meal, my sister-in-law Rose (Rob's mom and my brother Ron's ex-wife) came over and grabbed my hand and led me out of the building. She said that my sister Jackie wanted to see me. Rose and Jackie had developed a friendship. For some reason, I had never felt comfortable with Jackie, although she was always nice to me. Jackie was outside smoking with a group of other guests.

When Jackie saw me, she gave me a big hug. She asked me many questions. I tried to be cordial. I then returned to Marlene and Janet. Marlene asked for my address to send me some family information.

A few days later, I received a letter from my sister Marlene. Included was a family tree diagram that she had researched. That was when I realized that I had been an uncle 22 times, but I never met most of nicces and nephews. She also gave me information on everyone's birthdates and children's names.

After that, I called Marlene and visited her at her house. She showed me many old family photos. We discussed what happened on THAT DAY when we were separated as kids. It was a very rewarding visit.

About a month later, I received two phone calls. The first was from my sister Janet. She called to tell me that she had decided to quit smoking. I almost fainted.

"Why?" I asked.

She said that she finally realized that it was not healthy, especially since she had two heart attacks over the years. I congratulated her.

Then, a few days later, Rose called me. "Guess what?" she asked. I could not guess. She told me that she also decided to quit smoking.

"Is there something in the Racine water supply? Janet also quit smoking," I replied. I congratulated her.

RETURN TO NORTH CAROLINA

After nine years in Wisconsin, I decided that I was finally ready to move back to North Carolina. So, I called a friend who lived in Asheville and arranged a visit. I drove to North Carolina, and visited my friend in the Blue Ridge Mountains of western North Carolina. The scenery was beautiful, but I did not care for the busy traffic, narrow roads, tunnels, and hills around Asheville.

When I looked at the regional map, I noticed a small town about 20 miles south: Hendersonville. I had not heard of it before. I decided to visit. It was a small town with a population of about 12,000. It felt very friendly and comfortable, with a beautiful and active Main Street. I walked to the nearby public library, which was very modern, with several computer stations for public use. I visited a nearby county park with four nice tennis courts, several baseball fields, soccer fields, hiking trails and picnic areas. What a beautiful park! I then drove around the area to visit several apartments, and picked-up application forms. I might like to retire here.

I continued my journey eastward across the state to Durham. I visited old friends, played some tennis, hiked through the Eno River State Park, and walked on the first completed phase of the American Tobacco Rail Trail that I had helped advocate for many years ago. It was spectacular! After that, I drove back to Wisconsin.

Back in Racine, I decided that I did not want to move back to Durham—too hot and humid in the summer. That was tolerable when I was younger, but now the mountains seemed more comfortable for me. So, I mailed an application to one of the apartments in Hendersonville. I called to notify them of my application. However, they had no availability at that time. They suggested that I call back in a month or so. I did call the apartment, every month for five months, until finally in October, they had one availability.

I therefore proceeded to wrap up my stay in Racine. I quit my employment with the public schools, and notified my tutor students of my intended move. That was a bit uncomfortable, as I had developed close relationships with several students. My tennis friends gave me a nice going-away party. I moved to Hendersonville during the first week in November.

At the age of 58, I was planning to retire in Hendersonville, North Carolina. I expected to play tennis often, bicycle, hike the beautiful mountains, and swim below the many waterfalls. I joined a hiking club, and began hiking every Friday with a trail maintenance crew. I began tutoring students from the local high schools and from the local community college. I joined the local community college's Adult Learning Program, and attended many enjoyable education classes.

I volunteered with several non-profit organizations. I joined the local environmental organization, ECO (now merged with other non-profits to form the regional MountainTrue), and began volunteering to take water samples of the local streams, group leader for Adopt-A-Stream team to pick-up litter along local streams, and serve on the recycling committee. I also joined the Friends of DuPont Forest, and volunteered for litter pick-up activities, and at the annual festivals.

I joined the local Community Tennis Association, and began coordinating youth tennis activities, and helping to host the annual Apple Open Tennis Tournament. I joined the Friends of the Library, volunteered to help move donated books to the new library book store, and volunteered at the annual book sales. I also volunteered with United Way during the annual activities to help local non-profits and local schools. Finally, I volunteered with a local shelter for homeless boys, OnlyHopeWNC. This is probably the most rewarding for me since I reflect on how lucky I was to avoid that situation.

Reconnection

I visited Durham several times over the next few years. I re-connected with old friends. I bicycled on the fully completed American Tobacco Rail Trail—almost 30 miles long, and attended the ribbon-cutting celebration for the final phase of the trail—a pedestrian bridge over the six-lane highway, Interstate 40. I played some tennis, walked along the Eno River in the State Park, and swam in the adjacent old quarry lake (previously privately owned, but now part of the park). I attended a few annual meetings of the Eno River Association, and re-connected with other old volunteers.

Rose kept in touch with me, sending letters at Christmas. She notified me when I lost three siblings. I was 66 years old when I lost my older brother Allen Winsall (Tom Johnson)—he was 70. A year later, I lost my older sister Jackie Beth at 81 years old. Then, a year after that, I lost my older brother Ron Winsall (Butchie) at 76 years old. He had suffered from amyotrophic lateral sclerosis (ALS) disease for several years. His two sons, Rob and Tim, and our sister Marlene, cared for him.

When I was 70 years old, I received a Christmas card and note from my older sister Marlene. She wanted to re-connect with me. So, we started emailing each other, reminiscing about each other's lives. Very enlightening for me. She shared my emails with our younger sister Janet, who did not like to use email or computers. Then, Janet shared the email printouts with my older sister Kathy. Kathy called me—she was overjoyed to read my emails and to talk with me, and I was emotionally happy to talk with her.

Then, about a year later, my nephew Rob (my brother Ron's oldest son) emailed me that he was planning to visit friends and relatives in Charleston, SC, and wanted to visit me. His son Ronnie wanted to meet me. After his family visit, I decided to write this book. Over the next several months, I conducted several phone calls with sisters Marlene, Kathy, and Janet, and my sister-in-law Rose, along with emails with each one.

Since my first THAT DAY, I have been a truly lucky guy: I was adopted by two loving parents; I achieved a great education; I enjoyed a professional career; I met a lot of nice people and made some friends. I enjoyed several outdoor activities, including youth baseball and bicycling tours; and I am still involved in my passion—tennis. This has been a truly emotional journey, and very rewarding.

However, some things do not work out as planned. I developed stiffness and pains in both hips and lower back. A visit to an orthopedic medical doctor and x-rays confirmed osteoarthritis. Activity was not as much fun anymore. I gave away my bicycle, and stopped playing competitive tennis.

However, I continued to walk for exercise, and to coach youth tennis. I started regular visits to a chiropractor, massage therapist, and nutritionist. The treatments have helped to alleviate some symptoms, but not all of the discomfort. I am now undergoing adult stem cell, regenerative, biological treatments, trying to avoid hip replacement and back surgery. Wish me luck.

As a University of Wisconsin alumnus, I should close with two lines:

Always move "**FORWARD**" and

ON WISCONSIN!

ACKNOWLEDGMENTS

I WANT TO THANK MY PUBLISHER, Kira Henschel, for her many helpful suggestions in completing this book. I offer truly affectionate thanks for family memories and review comments from my three sisters: Marlene, Kathy, and Janet. I also affectionately thank my sister-in law, Rose, for her review comments and encouragement to complete this memoir effort. Finally, I thank my good neighbor, Marianne Hoppe, for her many questions and comments in reviewing my draft writings.

If you wish to contact me,
my email is rickburt9@gmail.com

www.ingramcontent.com/pod-product-compliance
Lightning Source LLC
Chambersburg PA
CBHW050822090426
42738CB00020B/3455